The WINES of ITALY

To David

Per ben vivere, bevi un

buon vino Italiano

Sheldon

9/22/76

The WINES of ITALY

A Consumer's Guide

SHELDON WASSERMAN

STEIN AND DAY/*Publishers*/New York

First published in 1976
Copyright © 1976 by Sheldon Wasserman
All rights reserved
Designed by Ed Kaplin
Printed in the United States of America
Stein and Day/*Publishers*/Scarborough House,
Briarcliff Manor, N.Y. 10510

Library of Congress Cataloging in Publication Data

Wasserman, Sheldon.
The wines of Italy.

Bibliography: p. 201
1. Wine and wine making—Italy. I. Title.
TP559.I8W37   641.2'2'0945   75-40475
ISBN 0-8128-1945-4

Mogliettina Mia

ACKNOWLEDGMENTS

In writing this guide, I received encouragement and assistance from many people. In all, there are too many to list. But let me take this opportunity to single out for special mention some of those who have done the most in helping me on this project.

To begin with, I'd like to thank Peter Morrell, of Morrell's Wine Emporium, N.Y.C., whose suggestion gave this book its birth. To Charles Gizelt, of Winefood, goes my heartfelt gratitude for his reading of and correcting the mistakes in the original manuscript. I'd like to thank him also for pointing out, "Don't say 'great Italian wine,' say 'great wine.'" If a wine is great, it is a great wine for that or any country. We don't say "a great Italian opera," so let's not say "a great Italian wine," but simply a great wine, without qualifier.

Mel Silverberg deserves a mention for his encouragement and editing on my original Italian wine article, which helped provide me with a basis for my further writing on the subject.

Thanks to Carlo Russo, of HoHoKus Wines and Spirits, whose bottle of 1943 Barolo showed me that great wines *are* produced in Italy and encouraged me to look further; he is also fond of saying, "It's what's inside the bottle, not outside [the label], that counts."

And to Lucio Sorre, of Frederick Wildman, who uncorked many a bottle to prove to me that Italy produces not only countless varieties of wine, but many great ones as well, my thanks.

To Roberto Ferin, my thanks for having introduced me to the Nebbiolo grape—one of the noble grapes of the world.

I'd be derelict if I didn't give recognition to the many importers who have opened bottles for me to taste and have put up with my many questions (and frank appraisals); of those, special thanks to

Philip di Belardino, of Mediterranean Imports; Guido Truffini, of Schieffelin; Barry Bassin, of Dreyfus Ashby; Aldo and Mario Daniele, of Daniele and Company (who also deserve a special mention for searching out and importing many of the better, lesser-known wines of Italy); Gerald Johnson, of Foreign Vintages, who gave me the opportunity to taste one of the rarest wines brought into this country—Recioto Bianco; and Paul Lardi, of Rolar Imports. Diana Masieri deserves thanks for reading the manuscript and making many valuable corrections. John Mariani, of Banfi Products, deserves recognition for what he has done for Italian wines in this country.

My thanks to Charles Castelli, of Cynar, for his assistance when I was working on the original version of the manuscript, and for sharing some older Barolos, Gattinaras, and Chianti Classico Riservas which proved again that great wines know no borders, but are produced in Italy as in France and Germany. Also, his enthusiasm for wine serves as a standard to me.

I'd like to thank Gene Beccali of Prosperity for giving me a chance to taste the very rare Picolit.

I must also thank T.B.A., of the Wine Bottle Museum, for his numerous tastings which provided me with opportunities to try hundreds of wines I might have not otherwise tasted.

And last, but not least (except for the aspect of size), I'd like to thank my little wife—for her typing, proofing, and editing, and her rewriting and writing of some parts of the book, which I think would justify her name as contributor, but she said no, so I would just like to say that she has added her touch to the book, which I think has added a lot.

While I have received suggestions, corrections, and information from many of these people, I take the responsibility for the finished product—including any errors it may contain.

CONTENTS

NORTHEASTERN ITALY

CENTRAL ITALY

SOUTHERN ITALY AND THE ISLANDS

INTRODUCTION

A few years ago, one could easily find good table wines for under $2 a bottle, and for special occasions a special wine for around $5. But this is no longer the case. Due to rising prices, good imported table wines at reasonable prices are becoming more and more difficult to find. While there still are good buys among the wines of France and Germany, they must be searched out.

Partly due to an increased demand for the better known wines, and partly due to worldwide inflation in general and U.S. inflation in particular, prices of wines along with most goods have risen dramatically. And projections are for a continuation of this trend, with occasional interruptions.

Therefore, to be able to afford good wine on your table, it is a good idea to learn about wines other than French or German. This book offers a pleasant solution to the problem by presenting information on the wines of Italy, overall the *best value* today.

Because of the relatively unknown status of Italian wines, demand for the fine wines of Italy hasn't really become widespread. It is, however, beginning to grow. Further, while the French franc is a hard currency, the Italian lira is soft, and the lira has fallen in value against the dollar, making prices of Italian goods cheaper in terms of dollars.

Another factor behind the relatively low demand for Italian wines is reputation, which has suffered from the actions of some unscrupulous producers. While unscrupulous producers can be found in all countries, including France, in Italy they seem to have made a bigger splash. Disregarding the many honest producers of Italian wine, people have chosen to focus on the dishonest ones. The reputation of French wines is helped on this score by government regulations (*appellation contrôllée*). Although one can make a good case for honest producers, negociants, shippers, importers, and merchants as being much more important than the wine laws, many people feel safer with such laws because the governments (are supposed to) guarantee the authenticity of the wines. In recognition of this phenomenon—reputation by government decree—the president of Italy, on July 12, 1963, issued a directive (#930) which commanded that a Comitato Nazionale per la Tutela delle Denominazioni d'Origine be formed with the goal of setting standards to regulate the quality of Italian wines.

DENOMINAZIONI di ORIGINE CONTROLLATA

Regulations were instituted which are subdivided into three groups:

DOCG—Denominazione di Origine Controllata e Garantita (Controlled and Guaranteed Denomination of Origin)

DOC—Denominazione di Origine Controllata (Controlled Denomination of Origin)

DOS—Denominazione di Origine Semplice (Simple Denomination of Origin)

In addition to the above, a DOC or DOCG may be granted a Classico designation when the grapes are grown in the original area of production. These regulations govern (1) the conditions of production, (2) the grape varieties, (3) the maximum yield per acre, (4) the physico-chemical and organoleptic characteristics of the wine and, (5) the area of production.

CONSORZII

The ideas behind the DOC regulations (DOS, DOC, DOCG) were based on the experience of the *consorzii*—voluntary associations of growers who met together and set standards for their wines. When the standards were met by a producer, his wine was awarded a seal from the *consorzii* which he could include with his label. This seal is normally found on the neck of the bottle.

Currently there are over fifty such growers' associations and the number is growing. As a corollary, the quality of Italian wine has improved and is continuing to improve. Just as the *consorzii* were a model for DOC, the *consorzio* of Classico Chianti was a model for the other growers' associations.

In addition to the Comitato Nazionale and the *consorzii*, all wine for export is checked, by sample, for quality and adherence to the standards established for that wine by the Istituto Nazionale per il Commercio Estero.

The manner in which Italian wines are named appears to have no rhyme or reason behind it. Barolo is a Piedmontese wine named for the town while Barbera, also from the Piedmont region, is named for a grape. Some wines are named for a region, e.g., Chianti; still others are given a fanciful name, such as Est! Est!! Est!!! However, upon close examination it isn't so incoherent as it appears to be at first glance.

Italy is the largest producer of wine in the world, with a total production that is slightly over 25% of the world's total. In this vast quantity is probably the world's widest variety, totaling over 700 grape varieties. Italy produces both still and sparkling versions of dry and sweet reds and dry and sweet white wines.

Fortified wines ranging from dry to sweet are also made. And there is a wide variety of apéritifs as well, including some very unusual ones—such as Cynar, a tantalizingly bittersweet apéritif made from artichokes!

Because of the growing world demand for wine, more and more lesser-known wine areas are coming into the limelight. Italy, the land of the vine, produces many wines worthy of discovery. It is my belief that when these wines are discovered, when they receive the recognition that they deserve, prices of the better Italian wines will appreciate dramatically. Consequently, the better Italian wines are worth searching out and laying down in your cellar to drink when they mature. Wines to lay down should not only retain their good qualities with age, but they should improve. Many of the Piedmontese, Lombardian, and Tuscan wines, in particular, meet this criterion.

Another facet of Italian wines worth pointing out is that vintage is less important there than it is in France, because of more consistent weather conditions. Its major importance on Italian wines is to denote the age of the wine (especially white wines). There are notable exceptions, however. Among these are Barolo, Gattinara, Classico Chianti, and the wines of the Valtellina.

Following the description of each region and its wines there is a list of most of the wines currently available in the United States. The wines are categorized by type and price range (based on current New York City prices). Some of the wines have an asterisk by them. This asterisk is a guideline. Although I have been drinking Italian wines for quite a few years, and have tasted many of these wines, I have not tasted them all. (Obviously, then, I cannot personally judge those I haven't tasted.) Also, producers sometimes slip a little or, for that matter, improve the quality of their product. The presence of the star, then, can be taken as my recommendation. Since taste can be highly subjective, it is possible that you will disagree with me, but I believe that some guideline, honestly arrived at, is better than none.

Now then, these are the *rules for the asterisk*: its presence is *an indication that the wine is a good representation* of its type. *No asterisk might mean only that I haven't tasted the wine*; it is unsafe to assume anything else. It will be noted that some types of wine, e.g., Bardolino, have no stars. The reason is, valuewise, you are better off with Valpolicella. Both of these wines sell for the same price, but while Valpolicella has a certain charm, Bardolino is quite common. This even includes the better ones such as Bertani or Lamberti. Some wines that are good representatives of their type are too high-priced—no star for them.

Certain wines rate not only one star, but because of their quality and price, they get two; these wines are the best buys.

I hope that you will find these guidelines useful. *Alla salute.*

NORTHWESTERN ITALY

VALLE D'AOSTA

Driving through the Great St. Bernard Pass from Switzerland, or the Mont Blanc tunnel or the Little St. Bernard Pass from France, we enter Valle d'Aosta, the northwestern corner of Italy.

This pine-covered mountainous region is bordered by high mountains—Mont Blanc, the Matterhorn (Cervino), and Monte Rosa on the north, and the Gran Paradiso range on the south, in particular. Valle d'Aosta is formed by a series of interconnecting valleys. The main one is the valley of the Dora Baltea River, with the others from that river's tributaries.

During the Carolingian era this region was overrun by the Franks. Later the dukes of Burgundy occupied Valle d'Aosta. Today there are over 300,000 French-speaking natives, the majority of the population. Although French is the major language, this region was never controlled by France. (The dukes of Burgundy occupied it before Burgundy became part of France.)

When the Italian merchants moved into the towns, the French-speaking population migrated to the surrounding countryside.

From Courmayeur to Pont-St.-Martin, the people still speak French. They work in the tourist trade, raise sheep, and live in chalets. Some of them continue to wear the old folk costumes.

The most characteristic feature of the vineyards in the Valle d'Aosta is that the vines are trained on pergolas on steeply terraced hillsides high in the Dora and other valleys of this region.

25

CAREMA

Carema,† the most esteemed of these wines, is made from Pugnet or Picutener grapes (the local name for the Nebbiolo), planted on rocky hillsides at a 2500-foot altitude. Only hillside vineyards are entitled to the name Carema, which is also the name of a commune close to the Piedmont border.

The history of Carema has been traced back to the sixteenth century, but its name has been protected only since July 1967, when it was granted a DOC.

Its 12 to 13% alcoholic content makes it lighter than Barbaresco or Barolo, its more famous cousins from Piedmont. Minimum aging requirements are four years, at least two of which must be in cask, prior to sale. With age, as with many other reds from the Nebbiolo, its color tends toward garnet. Its bouquet recalls roses (some say macerated roses[!], others, raspberries); and the flavor, although dry, is almost velvety. It finishes with an almost imperceptible bitterness. Carema is at its best after its fifth year.

Serve slightly cool with pork, veal, or lamb.

BLANC DE MORGEX

Blanc de Morgex is a light (10% alcohol), golden-colored wine that recalls herbs (some say alpine flowers) on the nose and palate. It is made from local grapes grown at altitudes from 3000 to 4000 feet. It goes well with fresh-water fish such as trout, perch, or pike.

† Generally listed as a Piedmontese wine.

DONNAZ

Donnaz is a wine with a 1000-year history. It is made near the communes of Donnaz, Perloz, and Pont-St.-Martin from no less than 85% Picutener grapes (Nebbiolo) grown at altitudes over 2000 feet. Freisa, Neyret and Vien de Nus grapes may be used up to 15%. These grapes have the lowest yield of any grown in Italy.

This light garnet-colored wine is smooth with a slightly bitter almond taste. DOC requires at least 11.5% alcohol and at least three years of aging, two in cask.

Serve with pork, veal, or lamb dishes.

CAREMA

Available for less than $5.

*Luigi Ferrando

BLANC DE MORGEX

Ranges in price from $2 to $3.

**CE.DI.VI.

OTHERS

Ferrando Vino di Aymaville Gamay

PIEDMONT

Piedmont is located on the same latitude as the Côtes du Rhône region of France, and the wines of both areas are similar: big in body and robust in character. The best wines require bottle aging.

This northwestern region of Italy is bordered by France on the west and northwest, and Switzerland on the north. Mountain chains stand to the north, west, and south.

Although Piedmont's viticultural output is sixth or seventh in volume of all the Italian regions, it is first in the output of *vini pregiati*, fine wines. The best wines are produced in the hills to the east and south of Turin, the region's capital, on both sides of the Tanaro River, and in the provinces of Vercelli and Novara.

Most of the better vineyards are found in a triangular area east of Turin, west of Milan, and north of Genoa. Generally, the reds are big, robust wines requiring lots of aging; but with age they really improve, becoming soft and velvety.

One of the finest districts is in the Monferrato hills to the north of the Tanaro Valley, cultivated since 1300. On these gently rolling chalk hills, south of the Po Valley, are orchards, vineyards, and castles. This vineyard area rolls through the provinces of Alessandria, Asti, and parts of Cuneo and Turin.

The finest grape of this area—and of all Italy—is the Nebbiolo, named after the mist *(nebbia)* which settles on the Monferrato and Langhe hills (on the south side of the valley) at vintage time. The hills become half hidden by the *nebbia*, and it is not unusual for the Tanaro Valley to be totally lost to sight. The Nebbiolo has been cultivated in Piedmont since the fourteenth century.

The Langhe hills, south of Alba, are chalk-covered with clay soil. This is the region which produces Barolo and Barbaresco, two of the greatest Piedmontese wines.

The Novara hills, in the northern provinces of Vercelli and Novara, yield the wines of Gattinara and Ghemme, considered by some to be in a class with Barolo and Barbaresco. What they lack in power they make up in elegance.

Approximately 90% of the region's output is red wine, with the remaining 10% white or *spumante* (sparkling), including the famous Asti Spumante.

ASTI SPUMANTE

Asti Spumante is produced in the provinces of Alessandria, Asti, and Cuneo from the Moscato di Canelli grape. Carlo Gancia, in the 1850s, was the first to produce this wine, which was sold as Asti, Muscat, or Italian Champagne, until the name "Champagne" became protected under a treaty with France. Today it is sold under various names: Asti, Moscato d'Asti, Moscato d'Asti Spumante, or Moscato followed by the commune name—di Cuneo, di Canelli, or di Strevi, besides the most common name of Asti Spumante.

The production of this delightfully light, sweet, fruity wine is protected by an association of growers, Consorzio per la Difesa dei Vini Tipici Moscato d'Asti e Asti Spumante, which awards a neck label to qualified wines. This label depicts the patron saint of Asti, San Secundo, mounted on a horse in blue, on a gold background. The neck label granted to qualified Moscato d'Asti wines bears a blue helmeted head on a gold background, or San Secundo, mounted in red, on a blue ground. This latter wine is commoner, cheaper, and sweeter than Asti Spumante, but little of it is seen in this country. This wine is a shade darker than the Asti, but is still pale.

Asti Spumante was awarded a DOC in July 1967. To qualify, the wine must be at least 7.5% alcohol but not over 9% and follow the traditional rules governing its production.

Asti is normally made by the charmat method (*autoclave*), although the firm of Contratto still makes a little by the *méthode champenoise*. In the charmat method, the secondary fermentation takes place in large glass or stainless steel tanks rather than in the bottle as required by *méthode champenoise*.

One reason given for preferring this method is that it requires only days instead of the months taken by the *méthode champenoise*, thus preserving the delicate muscat aroma which would be lost through the longer method. The actual and more mundane reason is to preserve the bottles of wine, which had a very high incidence of breakage, through exploding, when the *méthode champenoise* was used. Because of the high sugar content in Asti, as fermentation continues and the sugar changes into more and more alcohol, carbon dioxide builds up in the bottle to the point where it causes the bottle to burst. When the fermentation takes place in large vats, it can be controlled more easily. In the case of Asti Spumante, it is actually stopped before bottling, which takes place under pressure, keeping the bubbles in but the pressure at a safe level. Additionally, *autoclave* is cheaper.

The wine's pale color is artificially lightened to make it even paler. The aroma recalls grapefruit, peaches, apricots, or other fruits. Asti Spumante is a delicate, sweet, fresh, fruity, sparkling wine that goes well with fresh fruit or desserts. It is also excellent by itself, at parties or with late-morning brunch. It is delightful served in a wide-mouthed glass with fruit floating in it.

MOSCATO NATURALE D'ASTI

This wine is similar to Asti Spumante except that it is *frizzante* (lightly sparkling) instead of *spumante*.

BRUT SPUMANTE

This wine, first made 125 years ago, is produced from the Pinot Grigio and/or Pinot Bianco grape, using the *méthode champenoise*.

COLD DUCK

Some firms even make a cold duck, which was very popular in the United States. The only thing to recommend it is that it's cold. About the only thing it's good for is punch.

BRACHETTO

This wine is made from Brachetto grapes grown around the commune of Asti. It is cherry-red in color, with a floral aroma (some suggest roses), and is sweet on the palate. Serve chilled with strawberry desserts, especially strawberry tart. It also goes well with pears and the sweeter varieties of apples. Both still and sparkling versions may be found.

BAROLO

Barolo is produced from 100% Nebbiolo† grapes grown in the communes of Barolo, Castiglione Falletto, Diano d'Alba,

---

† Besides Nebbiolo, one of its three subvarieties, Lampia, Michet, or Rose, may be used.

Grinzane, Serralunga d'Alba, and Verduno in the province of Cuneo. This grape is ·planted on some 25,000 acres of the smooth Langhe hills, in soil of chalk and clay. This wine was a favorite of the monarchs of the House of Savoy in the nineteenth century.

Barolo is a big, robust, ruby-colored wine that is harsh and tannic when young. With age, however, it takes on a bright garnet color which eventually becomes *pelure d'oignon,* or onion skin (a brownish autumn leaf color), and its flavor is soft, smooth, even velvety. Its bouquet, of violets and tar (some smell faded roses!), requires four or more hours of air in order to open up. Even the older vintages of Barolo should be opened hours in advance; the writer recently had a 1947 Borgogno which needed no less than five hours to soften.

There is a custom in Piedmont, *'n fund 'd buta,* to serve the bottom of a partially drunk bottle of Barolo, which has been standing open for twenty-four hours, to an honored guest.

Barolo must attain at least 13% alcohol and be aged a minimum of three years (two in cask). With four years of aging Barolo may be labeled Riserva, and with five years, Riserva Speciale.

The Consorzio per la Difesa dei Vini Tipici Barolo e Barbaresco grants a neck label bearing the seal of a golden lion or a helmeted head on a blue background to those wines meeting its standards. Since more "Barolo" is sold than is produced, this neck label is an important indication of authenticity. (Its absence, however, doesn't necessarily mean that the wine isn't authentic Barolo. A good example: Borgogno, one of the best Barolos on the market, does not bear this neck label.)

In 1941, the Italian government awarded three wines the title of Vini di Categoria Extra; Barolo was one of them. (The other two were Barbaresco and Santa Maddalena.) In 1966, Barolo was granted a DOC. Current speculation is that Barolo will be one of the first wines awarded a DOCG, the most stringently regulated category.

Total output is approximately 500,000 gallons annually.

Barolo complements the same dishes as the big, robust wines of the northern Côtes du Rhône, and goes well with red meat roasts and game.

Great vintages: 1947, 1957, 1958, 1961, 1964, 1971.

Very good vintages: 1945, 1951, 1952, 1962, 1965, 1967, 1968, 1970.

No 1972 or 1975 was bottled as Barolo. It was all declassified; the vintage in each case was a disaster.

Worth mentioning, although not imported into the United States (at this time) are Barolo Chinato and Passito di Barolo. The former is a vermouthean type of wine, in that it is an old, mature Barolo which has been aromatized with spices and herbs. It is reputed to be a good digestive. The Passito, made from overripe grapes, is amber yellow, slightly aromatic, sweet, and 16% alcohol.

BARBARESCO

Barbaresco is an underrated wine produced from 100% Nebbiolo grapes grown in an area of the Langhe hills almost adjacent to Barolo. This growing area, four miles east of Alba around the communes of Barbaresco, Neive, and Treiso, is smaller than that of Barolo.

Like Barolo, more "Barbaresco" is sold than is produced and, again like Barolo, there is a consorzio which grants a neck label seal to those wines which meet its standards: the ancient tower of Barbaresco in gold on a blue background. A DOC was granted in 1966.

The output is approximately 100,000 gallons per year.

Barbaresco is dry and velvety with a brilliant garnet color. It is a rich, fragrant, and full-bodied wine. Although it ages quite well, it comes around sooner—that is, takes less aging—than Barolo. Also, it is less austere and less alcoholic, softer and more delicate.

This wine goes well with the same dishes as Barolo—game and red meats, although some experts suggest white meats and poultry.

Barbaresco must be aged for at least two years—one in cask, the second in bottle—prior to sale. With three years of aging it may be labeled Riserva, and with four years, Riserva Speciale.

Excellent vintages: 1964, 1970, 1971.

Very good vintages: 1945, 1951, 1952, 1957, 1958, 1961, 1962.

BARBERA

Barbera is produced from grapes of the same name in the provinces of Alessandria, Asti, and Cuneo. This grape is the most prolific in the Piedmont. Over 2 million hectoliters (53 million gallons) are produced annually.

Although mature at two, this wine requires a minimum of three years of aging to lose its tartness. It is a dark ruby red, with a full, dry flavor and a bouquet that is reminiscent of violets. (Some say it recalls black or morello cherries, but I have failed to detect this quality.) Its dry, strong flavor, like that of some of the commoner Côtes du Rhône wines, goes well with braised or boiled meats.

BARBERA D'ALBA

This wine is produced from Barbera grapes grown in the district of Alba. When young it is a deep ruby color which with age turns to garnet. DOC regulations require at least two years of aging prior to being sold. With an additional year and 13% alcohol, it may be labeled Superiore.

If from a good year, this wine has aging potential. It is dry and strong, and goes well with braised or boiled meats.

Very good years: 1947, 1955, 1958, 1961, 1964, 1967, 1971.

BARBERA D'ASTI

The best of the Barberas, this wine is from 100% Barbera grapes grown in the communes of Acqui Terme and Casale Monferrato in the provinces of Alessandria and Asti.

At times it is dry, at other times *amabile* (semisweet). Labeling and aging requirements are the same as for Barbera d'Alba. This Barbera has the most potential to improve with age.

Serve with the same foods as the Barbera d'Alba.

A *consorzio* grants a neck label to wines that qualify. The label depicts blue grapes superimposed on an old red tower.

Great years: 1958, 1961.

Very good years: 1947, 1950, 1955, 1964.

Although not generally available in the United States, Barberas labeled di Cuneo, del Monferrato, and d'Alessandria are produced. Barbera del Monferrato has been awarded a DOC; the others have not. In addition, a slightly *frizzante*, sweet version can be found.

GATTINARA

Gattinara is produced from Nebbiolo grapes (locally called Spanna) grown near the commune of Gattinara in the province of Vercelli. It can be from 100% Nebbiolo, but 10% Bonarda di Gattinara is allowed. The vineyards must be *on* sunny hillsides.

Wine from the vines planted at the foot of the hills cannot be labeled Gattinara; these wines are normally labeled Spanna.

Gattinara was awarded a DOC in 1967. According to these regulations, Gattinara must be aged for a minimum of four years—two in cask—and attain a minimum of 12% alcohol.

Its garnet color takes on an orange hue with age, and its dry, full flavor finishes with a slight bitterness. As with other wines produced from the Nebbiolo grape, its bouquet is reminiscent of violets. (Some say its perfume recalls raspberries when young and violets and roses with age.) Although not as strong as Barolo, Gattinara is more elegant and aristocratic with a most distinctive tannic taste. It is one of the world's greatest wines.

This elegant wine goes well with red meat, game, and truffle dishes. It also goes well with game birds, such as pheasant or quail.

Great vintages: 1952, 1964.

Very good vintages: 1945, 1946, 1950, 1958, 1961, 1962, 1967, 1968, 1969, 1970, 1971.

SPANNA

As Gattinara can be made only from grapes growing on sunny hillsides, those plants at the foot of the hills cannot be labeled Gattinara. These wines are normally sold as Spanna, the local name for the Nebbiolo, or else by a brand name, such as Santa Chiara. In addition to Spanna (Nebbiolo) and Bonarda, Vespolina grapes are also allowed.

Generally, Spanna lacks the depth and class of that from the grapes grown on the hills. The price, however ($3 to $3.50 a bottle, New York City), makes it worth searching out. The Spannas of Antonio Vallana are as good as or better than many Gattinaras.

This wine goes with the same dishes as Gattinara.

GHEMME

Ghemme is produced in the communes of Ghemme and Romagnano Sesia in the province of Novara from 60 to 85% Nebbiolo, 10 to 30% Vespolina, and a maximum of 15% Bonarda Novarese grapes. The vines are planted on hilly terrain with a sunny exposure.

Though similar to Gattinara, they lack Gattinara's class. Ghemme must attain a minimum of four years of age, including three in cask, and contain at least 12% alcohol prior to sale.

Ghemme is garnet-colored, with a hint of violets in the bouquet, and like Gattinara it has a slight bitterness in the aftertaste.

Great year: 1947.

Very good years: 1952, 1956, 1957, 1962, 1964, 1970, 1971.

Boca, Fara, and Sizzano are similar to, but not as good as, the Ghemme which is itself a lesser Gattinara. These wines are from grapes grown in the Novara province.

Grape Variety	Boca	Fara	Sizzano	Ghemme
Nebbiolo	45–70%	30–50%	40–60%	60–85%
Vespolina	20–40%	10–30%	15–40%	10–30%
Bonarda Novarese (minimum)	20%	40%	25%	15%

As a rule of thumb, the more Nebbiolo and the less Bonarda Novarese, the better the wine. Generally, then, the order of quality would be Ghemme, Boca, Sizzano, and Fara.

These wines—Boca, Sizzano, and Fara—must be aged three years, two in cask, and attain 12% alcohol prior to being sold.

The color is ruby, the bouquet brings up violets, and the flavor is full and dry.

VINTAGES

Wine	Excellent	Very Good
Boca	1959, 1961	1962, 1964, 1969
Fara	1957, 1967	1961, 1962, 1964
Sizzano	1957	1961, 1964
Ghemme	1947	1952, 1956, 1957, 1962, 1964, 1970, 1971

Of these wines, the only one generally available in the United States is Ghemme.

Ghemme goes well with steaks and chops, as well as lamb dishes. (Some experts suggest red meat and game dishes *after* the wine has acquired sufficient age!)

NEBBIOLO

Nebbiolo is named for the grape from which it is made, grown on sunny hillsides between Alba and Castellinaldo in the province of Cuneo.

The wine ranges in taste from dry to delicately sweet. Its subtle aroma recalls violets. When young, it is a ruby color which turns to garnet with age. The dry version is aged at least one year prior to sale, and attains at least 12% alcohol. It is suitable for moderate aging—and is at its best from three to six years old.

The semisweet (*amabile*) version should be served cool with dessert; it goes well with fruit. The dry (*secco*) type should also be cool when served. It goes well with white meats such as pork or veal when young, but when mature, as with Ghemme, it is recommended as a suitable accompaniment to steaks and roasts, although it sounds unusual.

The sparkling version is generally produced like Asti Spumante, by the *autoclave* method, and goes well with cakes and other pastries. A *frizzante* version can also be found. And a *nuovo* is now being produced—Bosca brings one into this country. This wine, being light and fruity, is similar to a Beaujolais in that it should be drunk within a year of the vintage.

CORTESE

Cortese, a dry, light, greenish-colored wine, is made from the grape of the same name grown on the Monferrato hills. It is light and refreshing with a dry, almost sharp taste and a delicate but fragrant nose.

Best when young, it goes well with fish and hors d'oeuvre.

The Cortese di Gavi (both semisweet and dry) is considered to be the best.

A *spumante* version is also made but rarely seen outside of Italy.

DOLCETTO

Dolcetto, a light, dry, pleasant wine, named for the grapes from which it is made, is usually dry (in spite of its name). Sometimes a slightly sweet, *amabile*, version can be found. There are two types: one, the most common, should be drunk when young; the other improves with a few years in the bottle. The more common one is at its best within two years of the vintage and is rather tired when it is four years old.

Dolcetto is clear, ruby red and has a subtle aroma. It is a good substitute for Beaujolais. The more common type can be likened to a Beaujolais, Beaujolais Villages, Beaujolais Supérieur, or one of the faster-maturing varieties like Brouilly; this type should be drunk young and cool. The other, more serious type, is more like a Moulin-à-Vent, in that it requires a few years of bottle aging.

Sometimes Dolcetto is labeled with a place name: Dolcetto d'Alba, delle Langhe, d'Ovada, di Strevi, etc. The one labeled d'Alba is the best; it is dry with a slight bitterness.

Dolcetto goes well with sausages or salami.

FREISA

Freisa, a garnet-colored, dry wine, is made from the grape of the same name. Sharp and ruby-colored when young, it becomes smooth and round when it is two years old. It has a distinctive aroma that recalls raspberries.

A sweet, sparkling version is made using the *autoclave* method. This version goes well with fruit and should be served cool.

Freisa is a good accompaniment to Bagna Cauda; it is a traditional combination.

A *consorzio* awards a neck label depicting black grapes superimposed on the tower of Asti in yellow.

It is not uncommon, as with many of the varietally labeled Piedmontese wines, to see a place name qualifier on the label: di Chieri, d'Asti, d'Alessandria, delle Langhe, etc. The most renowned Freisa is from a town near Turin—Chieri. Freisa di Chieri, with proper age, goes well with fowl, pork, and veal dishes.

GRIGNOLINO

Grignolino, made from the grape of the same name, is grown in the Asti-Alessandria area. At its best at from one to two years, it is too old at four. Some say there is a version which ages well, but I have never met up with this one.

This light, orange-colored wine has a pleasing aroma which seems to hint of roses. It is light in body with a dry, almost imperceptible bitter touch and a slightly sharp aftertaste. It should be drunk young and cool.

Grignolino goes well with poultry dishes or other light meats.

Sometimes the label will qualify the area of production—Grignolino d'Asti, d'Alessandria, etc.

Due to a vine malady, it is becoming rarer and rarer.

VERMOUTH

Vermouth, an aromatic wine, i.e., a wine base with spices added, was invented by Hippocrates nearly two thousand years ago when he made a sort of grog by adding almonds, honey, and gray amber to wine.

The name Vermouth has been traced to Alessio, mentioned as an expert mixer of Hippocratic wines in Munich. Vermouth derives from the German word *Wermut*, wormwood. (Absinthe, one of the ingredients used in Vermouth, is extracted from wormwood.)

In 1786, at the Piazza Castello in Turin, Benedetto Carpano produced Vermouth from a moscato base which was fortified by the addition of alcohol. To this he added an infusion of herbs and spices. The Cora brothers were next, then others copied them, and the Turin Vermouth industry was born.

At first, the Moscato di Canelli was used; today, however, wine from Sicily (Alcamo) and from Apulia (Locrotondo and Martina Franca) is used. To this basic wine, which can be a blend of several different wines from Apulia and Sicily and also Calabria, neutral alcohol is added. If the wine is to be used in sweet Vermouth, caramelized cane sugar is added for coloring. Then, a series of filtering and fining occurs. The wine is left to rest; then, it is filtered and fined again. Next comes aromatization—the infusion of up to ninety spices and herbs. The wine is then left to rest again.

Among the spices and herbs used are absinthe, angelica, bitter orange, camomile, cardamom, cardoon, cascarilla, cinnamon, coriander, cloves, dittany, gentian, hyssop, juniper, orange peel, quinine bark, rose petals, sage, sweet flag, thyme, and vanilla. Each house has its own recipe, which is a closely guarded secret known to only a few members. It is passed down within the family.

There are two styles of Vermouth: dry and sweet. The sweet Vermouth (Italian) comes in Rosso (red) and Bianco (white), the dry Vermouth (French), in white only. (The sweet Vermouth called Rosso is actually an amber color rather than red.)

The dry white Vermouth should be served very cold; the sweet white, cold with a twist of lemon; the red, chilled.

A bitter Chinato Vermouth is produced through the addition of Peruvian bark.

ASTI SPUMANTE

Generally available for less than $6 a bottle; a few are more expensive. The better-quality ones range from about $4 to about $6.

**Cora	Bosca, Luigi
*Calissano	Capra
*Cinzano	Castellano
*Fontanafredda	Cella
*Marchesi Spinola	C.E.V.I.
*Torre dei Conti	Contratto
Barbero	Cossetti
Beccaro	Fama
Bersano	Franco
Bosca, Giovanni	Franco Fiorina

Gancia

Gherzi

Graziola

Mabella

Mandia

Marchesi di Barolo

Martini & Rossi

Mirafiore

Perlino

Porazzi

Radicati

Ricasoli

Riccadonna

Rizzi

Sereno

Tavi

Tosti

Vallarino

Vallebelbo

Valli

Valtinera

Victori

Villa Pinza

KOSHER ASTI SPUMANTE

From $5 to $6.

Cinzano

Perlino

SPECIAL ASTI SPUMANTE

Less than $5.

Vallebelbo

MOSCATO NATURALE D'ASTI (frizzante)

Generally sells for just under $2 a bottle, and goes as high as $3.

*Moscalba

Cariba

Cossetti

Mandia

Opici

Vallebelbo

Zamboni

Zanti

LACRIMA CHRISTI

Usually available for $5 to $6, some are available from $3 to as high as $7.

*Fontanafredda	Martini & Rossi, Riserva
Barbero	Montelera
Bosca	Mirafiore
Capra	Porazzi
Cella	Tosti
Contratto	Vallarino
Gancia	Valli
Gherzi	

NEBBIOLO SPUMANTE

From about $4 to about $6.

Bosca	Marchesi Spinola
Capra	Mirafiore
Cella	Perlino
Cinzano	Porazzi
Cora	Ricasoli
Cossetti	Vallarino
Gancia	Vallebelbo
Gherzi	

BRUT SPUMANTE

Ranges from approximately $4 to just under $7.

**Cinzano Riserva Speciale
*Calissano Duca d'Alba

*Cora
Bosca
Franco
Gancia
Marchesi Spinola

COLD DUCK

From nearly $3 to almost $6.

Capra
Cinzano
Gancia
Mirafiore
Valli

OTHER SPUMANTES

From about $3 to just under $7.

Amerio Freisa
Beccaro Rosato
Mirafiore Royal Reserve, Extra Dry
Vallebelbo Grand Cru
Vallebelbo Pinot

BAROLO

Generally priced from about $5 to just over $6—some command more, with one selling for over $14. Others may be found for less than $3. Most of the better Barolos range from between $5 and $6.

**Borgogno	*Franco Fiorina
*Calissano	*Marchesi Spinola
*Contratto	*Oddero
*Fontanafredda	*Terre del Barolo

*Scanavino
Abbazia dell'Annunziata
  (Ratti)
Beccaro
Bersano
Bosca
Bosso
Buitoni
Carretta
Cascina
Cella
Ceretto
Conterno
Cordero di Monteze

Cossetti
Falletto
Franco
Gherzi
Giri
Graziola
Kiola
Marchese di Barolo
Marchese Villadoria
Perlino
Pippione
Rinaldi
Troglia

OLDER VINTAGES

Prices range generally between $8 and $20, obviously depending on a number of factors such as vintage, availability, and just how old it is.

    *Borgogno (including 1947, 1952, 1955)
    *Marchese Villadoria (1952, 1955)
    Marchese di Barolo
    Rinaldi

BARBARESCO

Generally from about $4.50 to $6, one commands nearly $10, and some are available for under $3.

*Borgogno
*Calissano
*Fontanafredda
*Franco Fiorina

*Gaja
Abbazia dell'Annunziata
  (Ratti)
Beccaro

Bersano

Cascina

Contratto

Cossetti

Franco

Gherzi

Giri

Marchese di Barolo

Marchesi Spinola

Parro di Nieve

Pippione

Oddero

BARBERA

Usually selling from just over $2 to just under $4, some go as high as $5.50; others are less than $2.

**Calissano (d'Asti)

**Contratto

*Borgogno (d'Alba)

*Brugo

*Marchese Villadoria

*Terre del Barolo (d'Asti)

Beccaro

Bersano

Bosca

Buitoni

Carretta

Cascina (d'Alba)

Castelli

Cella

C.E.V.I.

Conte Verde

Cossetti (d'Asti)

Fontanafredda (d'Alba)

Franco

Franco (d'Asti)

Franco Fiorina (d'Asti)

Gherzi

Giri (d'Alba)

Graziola

Kiola (d'Alba)

La Morra

Oddero

Opici

Perlino (d'Asti)

Ratti

Sarasino

Tenuta Galarey

Vallana

Valtinera

Zamboni (d'Asti)

GATTINARA

Usually from about $4 to about $6, some are available for as little as $3.50.

**Antoniolo
**Monsecco (Ravizza)
*Brugo
Avondo
Delle Valle
Fiore
Kiola
Travaglini
Troglia

OLDER VINTAGES

Prices generally range between $5 and $10.

**Antoniolo
*Brugo
*Troglia
Delle Valle
Travaglini

SPANNA

Usually ranges in price from around $2.50 to less than $4. A few command around $4.50.

**Vallana Campi Raudii   *Brugo
**Vallana del Camino   *Vallana Cinque Castelli
**Vallana San Lorenzo   *Vallana Montalbano
*Antoniolo Santa Chiara   Avondo

Avondo Riserva Speciale
Cantina Sociale dei Colli
  Novaresi
Delle Valle
Franco
Marchese Villadoria

Marchese Villadoria,
  Arcvino
Pippione
Sogno di Baco
Travaglini
Troglia

Umberto Fiore

OLDER VINTAGES

Prices go as high as the $50 range. (Vintages date back to the early thirties.) Those from the fifties go for around $10 to $15.

Vallana Campi Raudii
Vallana Cinque Castelli
Vallana del Camino
Vallana Montalbano
Vallana San Lorenzo

GHEMME

Usually around $3.50.

*Brugo
*Ponti
*Troglia
Delle Valle

NEBBIOLO

These range from less than $2 to over $4. The better ones are about $3.50.

*Giri (d'Alba)
Barbero Barberg (d'Alba)

Bersano
Bosca (Nuovo)

Buitoni

Carretta (d'Alba)

Cascina

Conte Verde

Franco

Franco Fiorina (d'Alba)

Gherzi

Marchese di Barolo (d'Alba)

Marchese Villadoria

Marchese Villadoria Riserva
   Cavour

Sarasino

Terre del Barolo (d'Alba)

DOLCETTO

Although most are under $3, the better ones are around $3.50. A few sell for less than $2.

*Franco Fiorina (d'Alba)

*Terre del Barolo (d'Alba)

Bersano

Bersano Tranquillo

Borgogno

Buitoni

Calissano

Carretta

Cascina (d'Alba)

Cossetti

Franco

Giri (d'Alba)

Marchese Villadoria

Marchesi Fracassi

Marchesi Rossano

Oddero

Pippione

FREISA

About $2.50 to about $3.50.

Balbiano (di Cheri)

Calissano (d'Asti)

Kiola Amor

Marchesi Spinola

Valtinera

CORTESE

Prices range from $3 to $4.

Beccaro
Cossetti
Franco Fiorina
Kiola
Marchesi Spinola
Vallebelbo (di Gavi)

GRIGNOLINO

Prices range from about $2.50 to about $3.50; a few are a bit more and a few others a bit less.

**Marchesi Spinola	Cossetti
*Borgogno	Franco
*Calissano	Franco Fiorina (d'Asti)
*Contratto	Gabiano
*Fontanafredda	Gherzi
*Marchese Villadoria	Giri (d'Alba)
Beccaro	Graziola (d'Asti)
Bersano	Marchese Villadoria Riserva
Buitoni	Cavour
Cascina	Perlino
Conte Verde	Pippione

OTHER WHITES

Prices range from less than $3 to less than $4.

**Calissano Castel Byria Pinot
*Contratto Moscato Passito (sweet)

Ferrando Erbaluce di Caluso
Fontanafredda Lacrima Christi (still)
Kiola Pinot Grigio
Orsini Penna Bianco
Vallana Bianco Greco

OTHER REDS/ROSÉS

While most are in the range just over $2 to less than $4, a few command over $10, and a couple are available for less than $2.

**Conterno Monfortino Riserva
*Castillo di Gabiano
Balbiano Malvasia Rosa
Bersano Bel Pais
Bersano Rosolino della Cremosina
Buitoni Albarosa
Cantina Sociale dei Colli Novarese
    Caramino
Cantina Sociale dei Colli Novarese Fara
Delle Valle Sizzano
Marchese Villadoria Pennanera
Marchese Villadoria Rosalba
Marchesi Spinola Brachetto Rose
Orsini Penna Nera
Orsini Penna Rossa
Zamboni Brachetto

VERMOUTH

Most are less than $3, although a few are higher.

Producer, Shipper	Sweet	Dry	Bianco	Others
Belroso	x	x		
Bino		x		
Bosca	x	x		
Capra	x	x		
Carpano	x	x	x	Punt e Mes
Cinzano	x	x	x	
Contado			x	
Contratto	x	x		
Cora	x	x	x	
Fama	x	x		
Gancia	x	x	x	Red, Gold
Gherzi	x	x		
Martini & Rossi	x	x		
Mirafiore	x	x	x	
Opici	x	x		
Pippione		x		
Porazzi	x	x	x	
Remondini	x	x		
Riccadonna	x	x		
Sarasino		x		
Sereno		x		Torino
Stock	x	x		
Toso	x	x		
Tosti	x	x		
Valentina	x	x		
Vallarino	x	x		
Valli	x	x		
Victori	x	x		
Zamboni	x	x		
Zonin	x	x		

LIGURIA

Liguria, the region of the Italian Riviera, runs from Monte Carlo to just beyond Portofino. It is an area of cargo ships, fishing fleets, tourism, and flowers. Most of the wine produced here is common and ordinary. There are, however, two exceptions, although they are not generally available in the United States at this time.

DOLCEACQUA

Dolceacqua (sweet water) is named for the town where it is produced. This wine contains up to 70% Rossese grapes and no less than 30% of others including Dolcetto, Massarda, and Vermentino. These grapes are planted on the hills above the Riviera from San Remo to Alassio.

This wine is a ruby-colored, light red wine with a strawberry aroma, a dry flavor, and an ever so slightly bitter aftertaste. Recommended with pork, veal, and rabbit.

Sometimes the label will read Rossese di Dolceacqua.

CINQUETERRE

The most famous Ligurian wine is Cinqueterre, so named because it is produced in the five lands (communes) of Corniglia, Manarola, Monterosso, Rio Maggiore, and Vernazza. Cinqueterre is sometimes labeled Bianco delle Cinqueterre, Rinforzato, or Sciacchetra.

The Rinforzato is dry and goes well with fish. Sciacchetra is sweet and a fitting accompaniment to fruit.

The Vernaccia and Rossese vines are planted on steep hillsides, between the rocky cliffs and the sea. Some of the terraced vineyards are very narrow, accessible only by boat, others only by rope or ladder.

Cinqueterre is made from semidried grapes. The *secco* type is golden yellow in color and has an intensely aromatic bouquet. The *passito* type, made from overripe grapes, is quite rare. It is an amber-colored wine that is lusciously sweet.

LOMBARDY

Lombardy, the capital of which is Milan, is the most industrialized region of Italy. The flat fertile plain of the Po Valley in the south presents quite a contrast to the rugged mountainous north, although the central portion with its hills and numerous lakes is a good bridge between these two contrasts. This is an area of poplars and willows, wheat and maize fields, rice bogs, and industry.

Besides its industry, and its rice, Lombardy is famous for Gorgonzola, the greatest cheese of Italy. This greenish-blue veined cheese is among the greatest marbled cheeses of the world, and on a par with Roquefort and Stilton.

The wines of Lombardy come from the Valtellina area—the best of the region—in the north, Oltrepo Pavese in the south, and the western and southern shores of Lake Garda (Colline del Garda, sometimes labeled as Riviera del Garda).

FRECCIAROSSA

Frecciarossa, the product of a single grower, Dr. Odero, comes from grapes grown in the village of that name near Casteggio in the Oltrepo Pavese.

Dr. Odero produces four different wines; all are estate-bottled, and carry the name Chateau Frecciarossa on the label. There are two whites—the dry La Vigne Blanche and the demisec Sillery. He also produces a crisp rosé, Saint George, from Barbera, Croatina, and Uva Rara grapes. But the best one is the Grand Cru red from, again, Barbera, Croatina, and Uva Rara grapes. This is the best Lombardian wine outside of the Valtellina. The Grand Cru red and La Vigne Blanche white are imported into the United States.

Great years (Grand Cru): 1947, 1961, 1962, 1964, 1967, 1969, 1970.

Very good years: 1945, 1955, 1956, 1958, 1960, 1968, 1971.

VALTELLINA SUPERIORE

Of all the wines produced in the Valtellina, the best ones are the Valtellina Superiore. These include Grumello, Inferno, Sassella, Fracia, Valgella, Villa (or Perla Villa), and one labeled simply Valtellina Superiore. These wines are from grapes grown on steeply terraced hills, facing south, some up to 2500 feet above sea level, on the northern bank of the Adda River. The best wine is from the lower terraces of the Alpine foothills, some 2000 feet up, east and west of Sondrio. Wines have been produced here at least since the fifth century A.D.

The wines are named according to the area they come from. The one labeled Valtellina Superiore is a blend of some of the others. Grumello, Fracia, and Valgella make up the better group. Although Sassella is generally considered to be the best, it and Inferno and Perla Villa are actually the lesser wines, but still quite good.

Those wines bearing a Valtellina DOC must be made from at least 70% Chiavennasca grapes, with up to 30% of the other varieties listed below. They must be aged for at least one year prior to sale.

All of the Valtellina Superiore wines must be made from at least 95% Chiavennasca (the local name for the Nebbiolo) and no more than 5% Black Pinot, Brugnola, Merlot, Pignola, or Rossola grapes.

The ruby color of these wines becomes garnet with age. The bouquet is quite pronounced and the flavor rather dry. Overall, while the quality is quite good, they lack the consistency and class of Barolo and Gattinara.

The wine must be aged for at least two years and reach 12% alcohol to be labeled Valtellina Superiore (including any of the individual names). The wines labeled Valtellina and Valtellina Superiore were granted a DOC in 1968.

Enologica Valtellinese bottles a Riserva (Inferno, Grumello, Sassella) which is aged longer prior to being sold and attains a higher alcoholic content. Only the better wines are used to produce this Riserva. It is a finer wine, capable of improving over longer aging.

Excellent vintages: 1947, 1952, 1964.

Very good vintages: 1954, 1957, 1959, 1961, 1969, 1970, 1971.

Generally, these wines mature in the following order: Valgella, Fracia, Inferno, Grumello, Sassella.

While Valgella is best with lighter meats such as veal or pork, the others will stand up to red-meat roasts or game.

The Enologica Valtellinese reputedly bottles a wine called Paradiso which is supposed to be similar to the Castel Chiuro Riserva of Nino Negri.

CASTEL CHIURO AND CASTEL CHIURO RISERVA

Nino Negri bottles a wine labeled Castel Chiuro, which comes in both red and white. The red, Castel Chiuro Riserva, is made from 100% Nebbiolo grapes that are specially selected from the best vineyard—Fracia, Grumello, Inferno, or Sassella—of that year. These wines are aged for a minimum of three years, two in cask. The remainder of the wine produced from that vineyard is labeled with the vineyard name.

The white is from Pinot Bianco grapes grown on the lower slopes of Negri's vineyard in Sassella. This is among the best white wines of Italy.

SFURSAT

Another Negri wine from the Valtellina worth mentioning is Sfursat. This wine, too, is made from 100% Nebbiolo. The grapes are picked during the normal harvest, in the fall, but they are then left to dry until January or February. After drying, they are crushed and fermentation begins. This wine is aged for at least three years, two in cask. The resultant wine is big and robust, with 14.5% alcohol, and requires four hours of air prior to drinking in order to open up.

LUGANA

Lugana comes from the Colline del Garda, south of Sirmione. This light, delicately flavored wine is made from at least 90% Trebbiano grapes. The vines are planted in clay and lime soil on the plains. Excavations have revealed that vines have been cultivated in this area since the Bronze Age.

This greenish straw-colored wine is the best white of the Lombardian Garda district and is a fitting accompaniment to the fresh-water fish from the lake.

Lugana was granted a DOC in 1967.

CHIARETTO DEL GARDA

Chiaretto del Garda, from the Riviera Bresciana side of Lake Garda, is normally a dark-colored rosé, although a lightly colored red can also be found. This wine is made from 50 to 60% Groppello, 10 to 25% Sangiovese, 10 to 20% Barbera, and 5 to 15% Marzemino grapes. Chiaretto del Garda must be at least 10.5% alcohol; to be labeled Superiore, 11.5% is required.

It is at its best, like the Lake Garda wines from Verona, when drunk young and cool. It has a delicate nose and a slight bitterness in the aftertaste.

GROPPELLO

Another wine from this region, Groppello, is named for the grape from which it is made. This wine is a ruby-colored, dry red that goes well with a steak. There is also a Groppello Amarone, produced in a manner similar to Recioto della Valpolicella Amarone (see Venezia Euganea). This is a much bigger wine and requires a red-meat roast or game to set off its rich flavor. The slight bitterness at the end adds a nice touch to this wine, which is similar in many respects to the Amarone of Valpolicella.

VALTELLINA SUPERIORE

Prices normally range from approximately $3 to less than $4. The Riservas are over $5, but less than $6.

GRUMELLO

**Rainoldi
*Bettini
*Pelizzatti Riserva
*Polatti
*Nino Negri
Enologica Valtellinese
Nera
ORFEVI
Pelizzatti

INFERNO

**Rainoldi
*Bettini
*Enologica Valtellinese Riserva
*Nino Negri
*Polatti
  Enologica Valtellinese
  Nera
  ORFEVI
  Pelizzatti

SASSELLA

**Rainoldi
*Bettini
*Enologica Valtellinese Riserva
*Nino Negri
*Pelizzatti Riserva
*Polatti
  Enologica Valtellinese
  Nera
  ORFEVI
  Pelizzatti

VALGELLA

**Nino Negri Fracia
**Rainoldi
*Bettini
  Pelizzatti

OTHER VALTELLINA WINES: RED

The prices on most of these are from around $2.50 to almost $4, although one is over $7.

**Negri Castel Chiuro Riserva
*Negri Sfursat
Enologica Grisum Valtellina
Pelizzatti Il Sole d'Alpi
Pelizzatti Riserva della Casa
Pelizzatti Valtellina
Pelizzatti Valtellina Superiore

OTHER VALTELLINA WINES: WHITE

These range from less than $3 to less than $4.

*Negri Castel Chiuro
Bettini Bianco Secco
Polatti Bianco di Montagna
Rainoldi Bianco

OTHER WINES

The range on these wines is quite broad: from under $3 to over $6.

**Frassine Groppello Amarone
Alberini Brachetto Spumante
Alberini Lambrusco
Alberini Lambrusco Spumante
Alberini Merlot
Frassine Groppello
Frecciarossa Grand Cru Red
Frecciarossa La Vigne Blanche

LUGANA

The prices range around $3.50.

Folinari
Ruffino

CHIARETTO DEL GARDA

Usually under $3.

Bertani Bertarose
Bolla Garda Rose
Cantina Sociale di Soave
Compostrini
Folinari
Frassine
Sanzeno Esportatione
Tommasi

NORTHEASTERN ITALY

TRENTINO - ALTO ADIGE

FRIULI - VENEZIA GIULIA

VENEZIA EUGANEA

EMILIA - ROMAGNA

TRENTINO-ALTO ADIGE

Trentino-Alto Adige, the northernmost region of Italy, is bordered by Austria to the north and northwest. This region of spectacular mountain scenery, with numerous lakes, rivers, and streams, is noted for its high-quality fruit and wine.

The best wine comes from the Süd Tyrol, as the Alto Adige is called by its German-speaking majority. The Adige Valley narrows in the north toward Austria and the Brenner Pass. Numerous castles and churches dot the hills. The valley is one vast vineyard, protected from the harsh north winds by the Alps. Forty percent of all exported Italian wines are from this area, most of them going to Germany, Austria, and Switzerland. These wines, many of them with German names, often have an undertone of almonds.

SYLVANER

The Sylvaner, which is grown around Bressanone and Nalles at an altitude of up to 2500 feet, yields a greenish yellow wine with a taste like that of ripe peaches. It is a good accompaniment to fresh-water fish, such as trout and perch.

GEWÜRZTRAMINER

Gewürztraminer, also referred to locally as Traminer Aromatico, is planted in Cortaccia, Egna, and Termeno. It is believed that the grape (Traminer) got its name from the town

Tramin (in German) or Termeno (in Italian) where the grape was originally grown. These grapes yield a dark straw-colored wine which has a dry flavor and an ever so slightly bitter aftertaste. It lacks the spicy elegance of its Alsatian counterpart. Drink this one with spicy fish dishes. It also goes well with strong cheese and curry.

PINOT BIANCO

The Pinot Bianco, also called Weissburgunder, is made from the white Pinot grapes. It is a golden wine with greenish highlights, with a dry, crisp flavor that goes well with fish, shellfish, or pasta dishes with cream sauces.

BLAUBURGUNDER

Blauburgunder is the name given by the German-speaking populace to the Pinot Noir. It is also bottled locally as Pinot Nero and Borgogna Nero. The best are grown near Bolzano, Caldaro, and Terlano. This dry, red wine has a full flavor and goes well with a steak or a roast.

CABERNET SAUVIGNON

The Cabernet or Cabernet Sauvignon, from grapes of the same name, ages quite well and is one of the best wines of this region. It is similar in quality to a Petit Château from Bordeaux.

Great years: 1947, 1949, 1959, 1964, 1969, 1970.
Very good years: 1957, 1971.

LAGREIN DUNKEL

Lagrein Dunkel, from the grape of the same name, is grown near Bolzano and Gries. It ages quite well. Recommended with white-meat roasts such as veal and pork. It is a dry red wine.

SANTA MADDALENA

Santa Maddalena was considered, at one time, to be almost on a par with Barolo. It is produced from Schiava, Schiavone, and Lagrein grapes grown on the hills near the town of Santa Maddalena on the Isarco River north of Bolzano.

This dark ruby-colored wine becomes orange with age. Its dry flavor goes well with steaks and chops.

There is also a Santa Maddalena Classico or Magdalener Klassischer Ursprungsgebiet.

PINOT GRIGIO

Pinot Grigio, also called Sonnengold or Rülander, is a light delicately crisp white wine that is flavorful and has character. This latter virtue is uncommon in Italian whites. Drink cold with fish or as an apéritif.

TERLANO

Terlano, a pale straw-colored wine, is considered to be the best white wine of the Alto Atesini. It has a subtle aroma, and is dry with a slight sweetness. It is made from Terlaner, Italian Riesling, and Pinot Bianco grapes grown on the hills north of Bolzano near the town of Terlano. Some other grape varieties are also added, but in minor amounts.

Although good, it lacks the character and crispness of the Pinot Grigio. Drink it well chilled with fish or other seafood.

A red Terlano is also produced, from Vernaccia, Merlot, and Lagrein grapes.

LAGO DI CALDARO

Lago di Caldaro, or Kalterersee, is a light ruby-red wine with a delicate berrylike aroma and an almondlike flavor which ends with a slight bitterness. DOC regulations specify a minimum of 85% Schiava Grossa, Schiava Gentile, and Schiava Grigia grapes with up to 15% Pinot Nero and Lagrein grapes allowed. A wine from selected grapes may be labeled Auslese, Selezionato, or Scelto.

These grapes are planted on the hills around the small lake, Lago di Caldaro (Kalterersee in German), near Bolzano. The Classico zone is near the lake, and wines labeled Classico Superiore must be from this zone and also attain over 10.5% in alcoholic content. The ordinary zone consists of seven small enclaves up and downstream. The vines grow at altitudes from 1000 to 2000 feet.

This wine should be drunk with fowl, pork, and veal dishes.

GRAUERNATSCH

Grauernatsch is a dry, strong, orange-colored wine with an aroma that brings up roses. It ends with a slight, pleasant, sharpness. This is a wine that goes well with sausages and other fatty dishes.

MERLOT

The Merlot is a ruby-colored wine with a berrylike aroma and a dry flavor. Drink with pork, veal, or fowl.

LAGREIN KRETZER

This rosé is one of the best of this type produced in Italy. It is from Lagrein grapes grown around the towns of Bolzano and Gries.

RIESLING

This white wine is noted for its charm and freshness. Both the German Riesling (Riesling Renano) and the Italian Riesling (Riesling Italico) are planted here, and used in this wine.

The Riesling can be quite good. It is a fitting accompaniment to fresh-water fish and is good alone as an apéritif.

ALTO ADIGE REDS

Prices normally range from approximately $2.50 to around $4.

> **Vaja Bonatti Grauernatsch Andreas Hofer
> *Kettmeir Cabernet Sauvignon
> *Kettmeir Lagrein Rosé
> *Kettmeir Merlot
> *Kettmeir Pinot Noir
> *Kettmeir Santa Maddalena
> *Vaja Bonatti Lagrein Dunkel

Convento dei Benedettini di Muri
Grieser Lagrein Dunkel
Convento dei Benedettini di Muri
Grieser Lagrein Kretzer
Convento dei Benedettini di Muri
Santa Magdalena
Kettmeir Lago di Caldaro
Vaja Bonatti Kalterersee Auslese

ALTO ADIGE WHITES

Prices range from around $2.50 to about $4.

**Kettmeir Pinot Grigio
**Vaja Bonatti Rheinriesling
*Kettmeir Riesling
Kettmeir Pinot Bianco
Kettmeir Terlano

VENEZIA EUGANEA

Venezia Euganea is similar in terrain to Lombardy, its neighbor to the west. The northern part is mountainous while the southern section is flat and fertile. Venice is the region's capital.

Rice, wheat, corn, mulberries, and beets are the crops of Polesine, the Po delta. Fruit trees, olives, and vines are grown near Lake Garda, south of Vicenza, near Padua. In the volcanic soil of the Berici mountains and Euganean hills are vineyards and peach orchards.

The vine in this area has a very ancient history: *Vitis vinifera* seeds from the Bronze Age have been found in the earthworks of Bor, near Pacenzo, in the province of Verona.

The major wines from Venezia Euganea are Bardolino, Soave, and Valpolicella.

SOAVE

Soave, produced in the Verona hills, is named for the charming walled commune east of Verona. It is reputed to be one of the best white wines of Italy. Soave is produced from 70 to 90% Garganega and 10 to 30% Trebbiano di Soave (Nostrano) grapes. Although granted a DOC only in 1968, its history has been traced back to the thirteenth century.

Those labeled Classico are from a strictly delimited area of production while those labeled Superiore must attain a minimum of 11.5% alcohol and not be sold prior to the July following the harvest. Soave is protected by a consorzio which grants a neck label depicting the Roman arena at Verona.

This lightly colored, delicate wine has a slightly almondlike bitterness at the end, and is noted for its freshness. It, of all Italian wines, can be likened to a white Burgundy because of its almondlike nose and flavor. (Some claim to detect the aroma of cherry flowers or elder flowers.)

Soave is at its best prior to its fourth year. Recommended with fresh-water fish, it also goes well, due to its dryness, with salt-water fish and crustaceans.

Bolla produces a Soave Spumante which is available in this country.

A very rare Recioto di Soave, or Recioto Bianco, is made from overripe grapes. This slightly bitter wine has a strong almond flavor that is luscious and rich. The only one generally available in the U.S. is bottled by the Masi estate, although the one by Pieropan can be found.

DOC allows the name Recioto di Soave with a minimum of 14.5% alcohol, or Recioto di Soave Liquoroso with a minimum of 16% alcohol.

A sparkling Recioto is also made, but is somewhat rare.

Drink with fresh fruit or after dinner by itself.

BARDOLINO

Bardolino is made from Corvina Veronese (50 to 65%), Rondinella (10 to 30%), Molinara (10 to 20%), and Negrara (up to 10%) grapes grown on the curve of the morainic hills along the western bank of Lake Garda, near the town of Bardolino.

Those labeled Superiore must be at least 11.5% alcohol and are aged a minimum of one year prior to sale. The Zona Classico of Bardolino encompasses the six communes of Bar-

dolino, Garda, Lazise, Affi, Costernano, and Cavaion. Bardolino
was granted a DOC in 1968. This wine is protected by the same
Veronese *consorzio* as Soave; look for the same neck label.

This light, ruby-colored, delicately perfumed wine has a
slight bitterness at the end. Some say it ages well, but that is
debatable. It is best when drunk young and slightly chilled.
Drink Bardolino with pasta dishes; it also goes well with roast
veal or chicken, pork, and lamb.

Occasionally a Bardolino Chiaretto (rosé) may be found. A
frizzante version is also made.

VALPOLICELLA

Valpolicella is similar to Bardolino, except that it is fuller in
flavor and deeper in color. The same grapes—Corvina Veronese
(55 to 70%), Rondinella (25 to 30%), and Molinara (5 to 15%)—
are used (up to 10% of other varieties are allowed); but they are
planted in heavier soil, in the hills north of Verona near, but
not on, the shores of Lake Garda. This wine has more elegance
than Bardolino, but it, too, is best when young and cool.

The one labeled Superiore is aged for a minimum of one
year and must be at least 12% alcohol. The designation Classico
is allowed for those wines from Fumane, Marano, Negrar, San
Ambrogio, and San Pietro. Valpolicella was granted a DOC in
1968. It is protected by the same Veronese growers' association
as are Bardolino and Soave. Consequently, the neck label shows
the same Roman arena.

The perfume of Valpolicella brings up almonds, sometimes
bitter almonds. This ruby-colored wine, usually light and dry, is
sometimes semisweet. Drink with pork or veal dishes, poultry,
and mild cheeses.

VALPANTENA

Valpantena is produced from the same grape varieties as Valpolicella, planted in the Valpantena Valley, north of Verona. The resultant wine is practically indistinguishable from Valpolicella. DOC allows this wine to be labeled Valpolicella-Valpantena.

RECIOTO DELLA VALPOLICELLA AMARONE

This wine is made from selected dry grapes, which yield only 40% of their normal juice. The word *recioto* comes from the Italian word *recia*, meaning ear. The grapes used are from the so-called ear of the grapes—the upper parts of the bunches. The lower and middle parts of each bunch are cut off before the grapes fully ripen, leaving the ears—the upper clusters at each side. These grapes get more sun and consequently are more ripened. The selected *rece* are then left on wicker frames to dry. After drying, which lasts into the winter, when the temperatures are near freezing, the grapes are vinified. Fermentation, of course, is slowed down by the cold weather. This wine must be at least 14% alcohol.

It is big enough to stand up to rich, spicy meat dishes.

Recioto della Valpolicella, an *amabile* version of the Amarone is also made. This deep garnet-colored wine has a big bouquet and a delicate, velvety, semisweet flavor with a slightly bitter aftertaste. Its bouquet reveals the dried nature of its grapes.

The only still one brought into the U.S. at this time is from the Masi estates. A Recioto Spumante also may be found. A Recioto della Valpolicella which contains 16% alcohol may be labeled Liquoroso.

PROSECCO

Prosecco di Conegliano is made from 100% Prosecco grapes grown near the town of Conegliano in the province of Treviso. It may be still, *frizzante*, or sparkling.

Prosecco di Valdobbiadene is also recognized by DOC. In this case, the grapes are grown near Valdobbiadene in Treviso.

DOC also allows the label to read Prosecco di Conegliano-Valdobbiadene if the grapes are from these communes and the surrounding areas.

There is a Classico zone, called Cartizze, around San Pietro di Barbozza, south of Conegliano. The *frizzante* may be labeled Superiore di Cartizze if it attains at least 11% alcohol. And the Spumante can use this designation if it is no less than 11.5%. These wines are generally the driest as well as the best.

The Proseccos are straw-yellow to light golden in color, with a vinous aroma. The *amabile* and *dolce* versions are quite fruity, with a varying amount of sweetness. The *secco* has a pleasant bitterness.

Drink the *amabile* and *dolce* with fruit, and the *secco* with fish or as an apéritif.

Valbona produces a still Prosecco as well as a Rosso del Veneto, both found in this country.

Carpene Malvolti also produces a *brut* which is excellent and very dry.

TOCAI DI LISON

Tocai di Lison is produced from the Tocai grape grown on the Valdobbiadene hills near the commune of Lison. This wine is a pale straw color with greenish highlights. It has a dry flavor and a slightly bitter aftertaste.

PIAVE

In addition to the Tocai and Prosecco grapes, the Cabernet and Merlot are also cultivated in this area. The Cabernet, Merlot, and Tocai make up what are known as the Piave River wines. These wines are similar to their counterparts from Friuli.

SOAVE

Most are less than $3, with some approaching $4. The better ones are over $2, however.

**Lamberti	Creazzo
**Masi	Frassine
*Bertani	Gancia
*Fabiano	Mirafiore
*Ruffino	Montresor
*Sartori	Murari
*Tommasi	Negrar
Antinori	Perlano
Beccaro	Pieropan
Bertelli	Prati
Bolla	Ricasoli
Bosca	Riva del Garda
Buitoni	Ruffo
Canova	Santa Sofia
Cantina Sociale di Illasi	Sangiorgio
Cantina Sociale di Soave	Sant'Anna
Castelli	Santi
Colombano	Sanzeno Esportatione
Conte Verde	Sterzi

Vallene   Villa Pinza
Victori   Zetagi
Vigna   Zonin

BARDOLINO

Most prices are less than $3; some approach $4. The better
ones are over $2, however.

Antinor   Murari
Beccaro   Negrar
Bertani   Paternella
Bertelli   Perlino
Bolla   Prati
Bosca   Ricasoli
Buitoni   Riva del Garda
Campostrini   Ruffino
Canova   Ruffo
Cantina Sociale di Illasi   Sangiorgio
Cantina Sociale di Soave   Sant'Anna
Castelli   Santa Sofia
Colombano   Santi
Conte Verde   Sanzeno Esportatione
Creazzo   Sartori
Fabiano   Sterzi
Frassine   Tommasi
Gancia   Vallene
Guerrieri Rizzardi   Victori
Lamberti   Villa Pinza
Masi   Zetagi
Mirafiore   Zonin
Montresor

VALPOLICELLA

Most are less than $3, with some approaching $4. The better ones are over $2, however.

**Lamberti	Murari
**Masi	Negrar
*Bertani	Paternella
*Fabiano	Perlino
*Ruffino	Prati
*Tommasi	Ricasoli
Antinori	Riva del Garda
Beccaro	Ruffo
Bertelli	Sangiorgio
Bolla	Sant'Anna
Bosca	Santa Sofia
Buitoni	Santi
Cantina Sociale di Illasi	Sartori
Cantina Sociale di Soave	Sanzeno Esportatione
Canova	Sterzi
Castelli	Tedeschi
Colombano	Vallena
Conte Verde	Victori
Creazzo	Vigna
Frassine	Villa Pinza
Gancia	Zetagi
Mirafiore	Zonin
Montresor	

RECIOTO DELLA VALPOLICELLA AMARONE

Usually ranging in price from around $5.50 to about $6.50, a few are under $5, and a couple over $9.

**Lamberti	Buitoni
**Masi	Fabiano
**Sartori	Mirafiore
*Bertani	Montresor
*Negrar	Prati
*Santa Sofia	Pule
*Tommasi	Sant'Anna
Bolla	Tedeschi

RECIOTO

Prices on these wines run anywhere from around $5 to about $12.

*Masi Recioto Bianco
*Masi Recioto della Valpolicella
Pieropan Recioto Soave

RECIOTO SPUMANTE

These wines are in the $7 range.

**Bertani Recioto Spumante
Bolla Recioto Spumante

PROSECCO SPUMANTE

In the $5 to $6.50 range.

*Carpene Malvolti Conegliano (*amabile*)
*Franco Valdobbiadene (*demi-sec*)
*Franco Valdobbiadene Superiore di Cartizze
    (*amabile*)
Alberini

PROSECCO, STILL

These are in the $3 to $4 range.

> Franco Valdobbiadene (*secco*)
> Valbona

OTHER REDS AND ROSES

Normally priced from about $2.50 to around $3.50; a few are less. A couple are over $4.

> Cantina Sociale di Soave Rosato di Verona
> Cantina Sociale di Soave Rosso di Verona
> Mirafiore Rose del Veneto
> Montresor Albarosa
> Montresor Frizzalba
> Montresor Rosalba
> Montresor Rustego Red
> Montresor Spumarosa (*frizzante*)
> Negrar Rose
> Ristorio Dry Red
> Valbona Rosso del Veneto
> Venegazzu Riserva di Casa
> Venegazzu Rosso
> Villa Maria Rosso

OTHER WINES

These wines range from under $2 to over $7.

> **Villa Maria Bianco
> *Carpene Malvolti Brut
> Bolla Soave Spumante
> Cantina Sociale di Soave Bianco di Verona

Montresor Biancalba
Ristorio Dry White

PRAMAGGIORE
AND PIAVE RIVER REDS
AND ROSES

While not all of these wines are strictly from these two areas, it seems helpful to group them under this heading as they are all from this general vicinity, and are virtually all varietal wines.

Prices range from about $2.50 to $3.50; a few are nearly $4 while others are available for less than $2.

    **Kunkler Cabernet del Piave
    **Kunkler Merlot del Piave
    Beccaro Cabernet Sauvignon
    Beccaro Pinot Noir
    Bosca Cabernet
    Cantina Sociale di Portogruaro Cabernet di
        Pramaggiore
    Cantina Sociale di Portogruaro Merlot di
        Pramaggiore
    Costozza Cabernet
    Franco Cabernet del Piave
    Franco Rosato Raboso
    Lazzarini Campo del Lago Merlot
    Lazzarini Lerive Rosso Cabernet
    Lázzarini Rosso del Rocolo
    Livio Cabernet
    Osvaldo Cabernet
    Osvaldo Merlot
    Quarto Vecchio Cabernet
    Quarto Vecchio Merlot
    Roncade Cabernet del Piave

Roncade Merlot del Piave
Sangiorgio Merlot
Santa Margherita Cabernet
Santa Margherita Castelvecchio
Santa Margherita Lison Rose
Santa Margherita Merlot
Santa Margherita Pinot Nero
Santa Margherita Rubino del Piave
Zonin Cabernet

PIAVE RIVER WHITES.

A similar situation here as with the previous wines (not totally Piave River wines).

Prices range from about $2.50 to $3.50; a few are almost $4, others are available for less than $2.

**Kunkler Pinot Gris
*Kunkler Tocai del Piave
*Quarto Vecchio Pinot Grigio
Cantina Sociale di Portogruaro Pinot Bianco
Cantina Sociale di Portogruaro Riesling Italico
Cantina Sociale di Portogruaro Tocai di Lison
Cantina Sociale di Portogruaro Verduzzo del Piave
Franco Pinot Grigio
Franco Tocai del Piave
Kunkler Verduzzo
Lazzarini Pinot Bianco
Lazzarini Tocai
Roncade Tocai del Piave
Sangiorgio Tocai
Santa Margherita Pinot Bianco
Santa Margherita Pinot Grigio
Santa Margherita Tocai

FRIULI VENEZIA GIULIA

In Friuli Venezia Giulia, famous for its dairy products and its ham, grapes are grown in the Udine and Gorizia hills. These plants yield mostly common red and white wines. The wines of Friuli have been divided into three DOC categories according to the area where they are grown: Collio or Collio Goriziano, from the hills of Goriziano; Colli Orientali del Friuli, from the hills of eastern Friuli; and Grave del Friuli, from the western hills.

Most of the wines from this area, available in the United States, are named for the grape from which they are made, although there are exceptions.

PICOLIT

The most famous of all Friuli wines—Picolit—although not available in this country, is worth mentioning. This deep-golden-colored sweet wine has a delicate perfume and a very distinctive flavor. It is a big-bodied wine, containing 15% alcohol. Picolit is best after four years of age, and goes well with strong cheeses.

This rare wine is difficult to find even near its area of production. The Picolit plant is suffering from a vine disease, and consequently is becoming rarer and rarer.

COLLIO GORIZIANO OR COLLIO

Collio Goriziano, or just Collio, is the name given to wines from that area made from Ribolla Gialla (45 to 55%), Malvasia

(Istriana [20 to 30%]), and Tocai (15 to 25%) grapes that are planted on the Goriziano hills close to the Yugoslavian frontier. This straw-colored, dry white wine must be at least 11% alcohol.

Wines made from 100% of one of the following grape varieties will indicate on the label the varietal name in smaller letters below the DOC Collio or Collio Goriziano.

Cabernet (Francese) is a ruby-red wine, dry on the palate, with a herbaceous aroma. It must contain 12% alcohol. A suitable accompaniment to cold roast beef.

Merlot is a ruby-colored wine with a herbaceous nose, a dry flavor, and a slight bitterness on the end. Minimum alcoholic content is 12%. Serve with white meats and poultry.

Pinot Nero (Pinot Noir), is similar in style to the Merlot. It must attain 12.5% alcohol.

Malvasia is a dry, straw-colored wine which must be no less than 11.5% alcohol. It is suitable for antipasto, poultry, or seafood.

Pinot Bianco, a straw-yellow wine with a delicate, almondlike aroma, is dry on the palate, and must be at least 12% alcohol. Serve with fresh-water fish.

Pinot Grigio has a light golden color, with a crisp, fresh aroma and taste. This wine must have 12.5% alcohol. Cold antipasto and fish dishes go well with it.

Riesling Italico is lemon-yellow in color with a firm dryness on the palate. Minimum requirement is 12% alcohol. This wine goes well with fish soup or seafood in sauce.

Sauvignon is deep straw in color. It has a delicately aromatic nose with a dry flavor. It must be no less than 12.5% alcohol. Serve with mussels, seafood in sauce, and shellfish.

Tocai is a lemony-yellow white wine. It has a delicate aroma and a dry flavor that ends with a slight bitterness, which is pleasant and adds character to the wine. It must be at least 12% alcohol.

Traminer must also be 12% alcohol. It is deep yellow with an aromatic nose and flavor. Serve with highly seasoned seafood and hors d'oeuvre.

COLLI ORIENTALI DEL FRIULI

Wines produced from grapes grown on the eastern Friuli hills in the Udine province may use the DOC Colli Orientali del Friuli. All of these wines are varietally labeled. The wine must be made from no less than 90% of the variety named.

Picolit, discussed above, is covered by this DOC.

Cabernet (Cabernet Francese or Cabernet Sauvignon) is a dry, ruby-red wine containing 12% alcohol, minimum. It is at its best after five years.

Merlot is a dry, ruby-red wine which is at its best after four years. It contains a minimum of 12% alcohol.

Pinot Nero is a dry, ruby-red wine with a slightly bitter aftertaste. It must attain no less than 12% alcohol.

Refosco (Nostrano or Peduncolo Rosso), a purplish dry wine, has a vinous aroma and a touch of bitterness at the end. It must be 12% alcohol, minimum. This wine goes well with white-meat roasts.

Pinot Bianco must be at least 12% alcohol. It is medium straw in color with a smooth, dry flavor and a delicate aroma.

Pinot Grigio is similar to the Pinot Bianco, except that it is crisper. It also must attain 12% alcohol.

Riesling Renano is pale yellow in color and has a full, dry flavor. It must be at least 12% alcohol.

Sauvignon, of 12% minimum alcohol, is pale gold in color with a delicate, aromatic nose and a dry flavor.

Tocai Friulano has a medium straw color and a delicate aroma. Its flavor is rich and dry. Like the others, this must be 12% alcohol, minimum.

Verduzzo Friulano is golden in color and ranges from dry to sweet. Regardless of the degree of sweetness, the wine must be 12% alcohol. The aroma is fruity with the most intense nose on the sweet version, Ramandolo. This latter is made from semidried grapes. Drink with fresh fruit.

Ribolla is light straw in color, with a perfumy aroma, and a dry flavor. It also must attain 12% alcohol under DOC regulations. Serve with antipasto, fresh-water fish.

In general, these wines go with the same dishes as their counterparts in Collio Goriziano.

The term Riserva can be used on the label of the four reds and the Picolit if the wine has been aged for no less than two years prior to its sale.

GRAVE DEL FRIULI

The Grave del Friuli DOC applies to grapes grown on the gravelly soil of the western Friuli hills in the Udine and Pordenone. Like the varietally labeled wines of the Colli Orientali DOC, these wines must be made from no less than 90% of the variety named. The name will be smaller and appear below the DOC name.

As a general rule, these wines go with the same foods as their counterparts in the other Friuli areas.

The Grave del Friuli wines are Cabernet (red), Merlot (red), Refosco Nostrano or Peduncolo Rosso (red), Pinot Bianco (white), Pinot Grigio (white), Tocai (white), and Verduzzo Friulano (white).

These wines must all, with the exception of the Pinot Bianco, attain a minimum of 11% alcohol; the Pinot Bianco must be 11.5%.

The Tocai is reputed to be the best white wine of the Friuli region, but, not so; the best white is the Pinot Grigio, although even this lacks distinction. While the Merlot is reputed to be the best red of the region, the Cabernet is better, and even this wine is less distinguished than its counterpart in the Alto Adige.

RED WINES

Prices range from about $2.50 to about $3.50.

*Angoris Cabernet
*Collavini Cabernet
Angoris Merlot
Angoris Mont Quarin Red
Angoris Pinot Nero Riserva
Angoris Refosco Riserva
Cantina Sociale Coop. Grave del Friuli
  Cabernet
Cantina Sociale Coop. Grave del Friuli
  Merlot
Collavini Merlot
Collavini Pinot Nero
Modolet Rose Spumante

WHITE WINES

Prices range from about $2.50 to about $3.50.

**Angoris Pinot Grigio
**Angoris Traminer
**Collavini Pinot Grigio
*Collavini Tocai
Angoris Mont Quarin Blanc
Angoris Pinot Bianco
Angoris Riesling
Angoris Tocai
Cantina Sociale Coop. Grave del Friuli
  Pinot Grigio

Cantina Sociale Coop. Grave del Friuli
  Verduzzo
Collavini Pinot Bianco
Gradnik Collio Sauvignon
Modolet Brut Spumante

EMILIA-ROMAGNA

Emilia-Romagna is the gastronomic region of Italy. Bologna, the capital, and Modena contain more good restaurants than any other Italian cities of comparable size. The rich, hearty cuisine of this region is set off well by its light wines.

Emilia-Romagna is a region of wide fields, mulberries, maples, and elms—an area of mixed cultivation, with vines interspersed among other crops; where vines can be seen growing under elm trees or clinging to tall posts. Many of the vines are planted in the plains.

The region's most noted wine, Lambrusco, is best served young and cool. There are many types of Lambrusco, and they are usually named for the predominant sub-variety of that grape. Most Lambrusco sold in this country is non-DOC.

A *consorzio* grants a neck label—a white cock and grapes, or a man and woman treading grapes—to those wines which qualify.

LAMBRUSCO

The most esteemed of the Lambruscos, Lambrusco di Sorbara, is made from a minimum of 60% Lambrusco di Sorbara grapes, grown in ten communes in the province of Modena. Up to 40% Lambrusco Salamino grapes are allowed. This ruby-colored wine may be dry or semisweet. According to DOC requirements, it must be no less than 11% alcohol.

It has a delicate, fruity perfume that some say recalls violets,

91

and a natural effervescence. When poured, a rich froth appears in the glass, which soon disappears (the froth, not the glass) and leaves a slight prickle on the tongue. This is characteristic of all Lambruscos. Some claim to detect a bitterness in this wine, but it escapes me.

This wine is suggested as a suitable accompaniment to rich, hearty dishes, but I think it would be best as a punch with fruit added to serve at parties or on summer afternoons. (Veronelli, the noted Italian wine authority, suggests serving this wine with river trout cooked in butter and sage!)

The Lambrusco Salamino di Santa Croce, grown in eleven communes in the Modena province, must be made from at least 90% Lambrusco Salamino, so called because the grapes are sausage-shaped. Up to 10% of other Lambrusco varieties and Uva d'Oro are allowed. DOC specifies a minimum of 11% alcohol.

This ruby-colored wine has a vinous and fruity aroma and may be either dry or semisweet. Like all Lambruscos, it has a slight prickle.

Lambrusco Grasparossa di Castelvetro must be made from at least 85% Lambrusco Grasparossa grapes; up to 15% of other Lambrusco varieties and Uva d'Oro is allowed. The name Grasparossa refers to the red stalks of the vines. The grapes are grown in fourteen communes around Castelvetro in the province of Modena. DOC specifies no less than 10.5% alcohol.

This ruby-colored wine has a vinous aroma and a prickle on the palate.

ALBANA DI ROMAGNA

Albana di Romagna, granted a DOC in 1967, is made from 100% Albana grapes. The vines grow almost to the Adriatic Sea, on the hills from Rimini to Bologna in the provinces of Bologna, Cesena, Faenza, Forli, and Imola.

This light golden wine has a distinctive aroma and may be dry *(secco)* or semisweet *(amabile)*. The dry version, which is less common, has a touch of sweetness. It is less golden in color than the sweeter version. The *secco* must be at least 12% alcohol, while the *amabile* must be at least 12.5%.

This wine is protected by the same *consorzio* as Lambrusco, which grants a neck label depicting a white cock and a bunch of grapes on a red background, or a man and a woman treading grapes. Albana is also protected by the DOC.

The dry version goes well with seafood and pasta dishes, while the semisweet is best with fruit or dessert.

A *spumante* version can be found—but not in the United States.

SANGIOVESE DI ROMAGNA

Sangiovese di Romagna is from 100% Sangiovese grapes grown in communes in the provinces of Bologna, Forli, and Ravenna. This brilliant, ruby-colored wine has a vinous scent that hints of violets. It is dry and slightly tannic on the palate, with an almost imperceptible bitterness at the end.

A *consorzio* grants a neck label to qualified wines. Since it is the same association as Albana di Romagna, it is the same label.

DOC requires a minimum alcoholic content of 11.5%, and allows the designation Riserva if the wine has been aged two years prior to sale.

This wine goes well with steak or chops and sharp cheeses.

SCANDIANO BIANCO

Scandiano Bianco, a pale straw-colored wine of 11% alcohol, can be dry or sweet, still or sparkling. Drink it very cold with fish.

TREBBIANO DI ROMAGNA

Trebbiano di Romagna, from the grape of the same name, is a light white wine that ranges from dry to semisweet. This grape is a native of Emilia-Romagna; its name comes from the Val di Trebbia, south of Piacenza.

Trebbiano di Romagna is a good accompaniment to poultry and fish dishes.

LAMBRUSCO

Prices are generally about $2 to $2.50; a few are more expensive, while some can be found for less than $2.

Allini	Gioia
Baroncini	Interprovinciale
Barone	Leonard (Zetagi)
Beccaro	Lini
Bersano	Mandia
Bon Sol	Mazzolini
Bosca	Mazzoni
Castel Ruboun	Medici
Castellano	Opici
Cella	Pavan
Chiarli	Perlino
Conte Verde	Riunite
Conti	Riunite Cristallo
Creazzo	Ruffino Contesa
Donelli	Sant'Anna
Fratelli	Sant'Anna (*spumante*)
Fabiano	Sardelli Dragone
Gerelli	Zetagi
Giacobazzi	Zonin

SCANDIANO BIANCO

Prices are generally between $2 and $3.

Castel Ruboun
Donelli
Medici
Riunite

SANGIOVESE DI ROMAGNA

Prices are about $3.

**Pasolini
Carradora
Corvio

ALBANA DI ROMAGNA

Prices are about $3.

Carradora
Corvio
Pasolini

TREBBIANO DI ROMAGNA

Prices are in the $2.50 range.

Carradora
Chiarli

Corvio
Donelli
Sant'Anna
Zonin

OTHER WINES

Prices are in the $2 to $3 range.

Baroncini Bianco
Baroncini Rosato
Baroncini Rosso
Giacobazzi Bianco
Giacobazzi Rosato
Gioia Rose
Medici Lambrusco Rose
Riunite Cristallo Bianco
Riunite Cristallo Rosato
Riunite Rosato
Sardelli Dragone Lamblanco
Zonin Lambrusco Rose

CENTRAL ITALY

TUSCANY

CHIANTI

Tuscany, a region with a rugged, stony landscape, of mountains and hills, plains and vast forests, and countless castles, is the region of Chianti and the land of the Gallo Nero. This black cockerel is the symbol of Classico Chianti, awarded to qualified wines by the Classico *consorzio*.

Tuscany has a long viticultural history. By the ninth century B.C., the Etruscans were cultivating the vine and practicing the art of winemaking. But very little is known of the Tuscan wines of the Roman period.

In the dark ages, the hills of Tuscany were covered with vines, planted by the monks, most likely, who took shelter in this area. The red wine of Tuscany was then called Vermiglio for its bright scarlet color. It is described as having a scent of violets and irises.

This was a region abounding in game, and hunting was a popular activity. Bird calls, the blast of hunting horns, the shouts of the hunters—the sounds of the chase—echoed throughout the land. It is believed that the name Chianti derives from the Latin word *clangor*, meaning the sound of the trumpet, or the calls of birds.

It was apparently used first for the region, later for the wine. The first known use of the name Chianti in print appears in a document dating from 790 A.D., in the possession of the abbey of San Bartolomeo in Ripoli. The document confirms the donation of lands *in Chianti cum integro salingo.* Another old document—of July 14, 1211—also uses the name Chianti in referring to an area of land. This time, in describing the details of a sale of properties, from Ugo Ranieri and Bernardino, sons of Ugo Fortibraccio della Val Curiale, to Pietro di San Giusto a Rentannano.

Chianti makes its first appearance officially, so far as we know, in a book of Montaperti in 1260 A.D.

It isn't until the late fourteenth century that we find the name used to refer to a wine. Up until that time, the red wine of Tuscany had been called *Vermiglio,* the white wine, *Trebbiano.*

Francesco Datini and Bartolomeo Cambioni, in their book *Campagnia del Banco,* state that Francescho di Marcho e Stoldo di Lorenzo owed "three florins, twenty-six soldi, and eight denarri" to Piero di Tino Riccio for six casks of *white* "Chianti" wine. This book, in the Datini Archives in Prato, dates from December 16, 1398.

Over the course of the next two centuries, the name Chianti was occasionally used for both the red and the white wine of this area. But the name didn't really catch on until the seventeenth century and has since come to be practically a household word.

It has been over a hundred years since Baron Ricasoli discovered the mixture of grapes that has been used in Chianti ever since: 50 to 80% Sangiovese, 10 to 30% Trebbiano, 10 to 30% Malvasia, 10 to 30% Canaiolo, and 5% other grapes such as Colorino. (Colorino is recommended for wines made by the *governo* system, as most Chianti is.)

Baron Ricasoli is also credited with the introduction of new techniques of cultivation as well as the discovery of the *governo all'uso Toscano.*

The *governo* was actually first suggested in the fourteenth century by Francesco di Giovanni di Durante and Ruberto di

Guido Bernardi. Durante suggested that the juice of dried white grapes, which had been boiled in a cauldron, be added to the wine. Bernardi suggested the use of black grapes and no heat.

This system employs a contrived seondary fermentation, which imparts a freshness to the wine. Some grapes, the best bunches, selected and gathered prior to the vintage, are left to dry on *cannicci* (wicker frames). The rich must from these grapes (5 to 10%) is then added to the other, racked, wine immediately following the first fermentation.

This addition causes an early malolactic fermentation (the conversion of malic acid to lactic acid), which lasts for fifteen to twenty days. Wines made by the *governo* system are meant to be drunk young. Usually they are sold in *fiaschi*, the bottles covered with straw baskets, although this style of bottle will be seen less and less in the future as it has become too expensive, the baskets being hand-woven. This type of bottle holds more wine while presenting less of a surface to the air by volume, thus preserving the freshness imparted to the wine via the *governo*.

The *fiaschi* were first used toward the middle of the fifteenth century. The original purpose was to keep the wine cool; Tuscany has some very hot summers. The workers would bring the wine from the cellar to the fields to drink with lunch, and the sun would warm it up. They discovered that shielding it from the sun's rays by wrapping it in straw would keep it cooler.

The technique of glassmaking had been brought to an advanced stage in Florence by this time. During the fifteenth century, the straw-covered Tuscan flasks came into use. It was discovered that these baskets had the further advantage of making it easier to transport the flasks of wine to market, by making them less likely to break.

The *governo all'uso Chianti* takes place at the end of the year. A second *governo* (*rigoverno*) can take place in March or

April. The idea behind the *rigoverno* is to increase the glycerine content of the wine to give it more roundness and more freshness.

In 1376, the Chianti League was formed. The purpose of the league was to hold off the attacking forces from Siena long enough for the Florentines to arm themselves. This league also formulated certain rules regarding the production of Chianti in order to protect the reputation of their popular wine. The first regulations were issued by the league in 1384. Reforms were added, at least through the first half of the next century.

The black cockerel on a golden background was chosen as the symbol of the league, and today is awarded to those wines that meet the standards of the Consorzio per la Difesa del Vino Tipico di Chianti. This *consorzio* of Classico Chianti, founded in 1924, persuaded the government to protect the Zona Classica, some 200 square miles, stretching from just south of Florence to slightly north of Siena, and its name. This area corresponds to the region of the fourteenth-century Chianti League.

The Classico district, of approximately 173,000 acres, covers the communes of Castellina, Gaiole, Radda, and portions of other communes in the provinces of Florence and Siena. The soil of the Classico district is clay schist with flint and limestone and pebbly, sandy topsoil. A ministerial decree of July 1932 defined the Classico area and in addition allowed the use of the name Chianti without the Classico designation to other Tuscan provinces.

With the advent of government DOC regulations, Classico Chianti was awarded a DOC. Other Chianti districts to be awarded DOC are—Colli Aretini, Colli Senesi, Colli Fiorentini, Colline Pisane, Montalbano, and Rufina.

According to DOC regulations, Chianti cannot be sold prior to March following the vintage.

Chianti is ruby-red in color tending to garnet with age. The bouquet is reminiscent of violets, more noticeable in Classico than in other Chiantis. The flavor is dry and slightly tannic, turning soft and velvety with age.

Wines of the *governo* are lively and refreshing. They must attain a minimum of 11.5% alcohol, while those labeled Classico must be 12%.

Chianti that has been aged for two years and contains at least 12% alcohol can be labeled Vecchio. A Classico with at least 12.5% alcohol, which has been aged for a minimum of three years, may be labeled Riserva. Generally, Classico Riservas are the best wines to lay away, as they age well up to a decade and more. Governo Chianti does not age well at all.

Among the better vintages of the Zona Classica:

Great years: 1958, 1971.

Very good years: 1947, 1949, 1952, 1955, 1957, 1962, 1964, 1967, 1968, 1969, 1970.

There are 2.6 million gallons of Classico and 7.9 million gallons of all other *consorzio* Chianti produced annually.

The other *consorzii* are:

Chianti Colli Aretini. This area, east of the Classico zone, produces wine that is harder and more acidic than other Chiantis. It is usually drunk within a year of the vintage. The *consorzio* grants a neck label bearing a chimera.

Chianti Colli Fiorentini, Chianti del Putto, is from grapes grown between Florence and the Zona Classica. This wine, with its neck label depicting a cherub, resembles Classico; it is worth laying down for a few years, as it will improve.

Chianti Colli Senesi is from the area just south of the Zona Classica; it is best when young. Its neck label depicts Romulus and Remus with the she-wolf.

Chianti Colline Pisane, with a centaur on its neck label, is not highly regarded. This wine from the Pisan hills may well be ignored except as a curiosity. If you do acquire a bottle of it, drink it young.

Chianti dei Colli Empolesi is similar to Classico Chianti. Its neck label shows a bunch of grapes.

Chianti delle Colline Val d'Elsa, from the Elsa Valley, resembles Senesi and should also be drunk young. The *consorzio* awards a neck label depicting a red Florentine lily on a gold background.

Chianti Montalbano Pistoiese, showing the tower of Montalbano on the neck label, is from the area between Pistoia and Florence. With age, this wine acquires a distinctive violet scent. It is worth laying down to age.

Chianti Rufina is fuller than other Chiantis. Some undergo two *governo* processes. Like Colli Fiorentini, the neck label pictures a *putto.* Some experts suggest that this wine has an aroma of fruit.

Among the better vintages of Chianti:

Great year: 1958.

Very good years: 1945, 1951, 1954, 1955, 1962, 1970, 1971.

The Classico *consorzio,* as mentioned, grants a neck label picturing a black cockerel on a gold background. This symbol is bordered by different colors according to the length of time the wine has been aged—a red border for less than two years; a silver border, two years of aging; and a gold border for three years.

The best Chiantis, and the best for aging, are the Classico Riservas. These wines, with proper age, are a good substitute at a considerably lower price for the clarets of Bordeaux. Like the more famous clarets, they have an elegance and delicacy expected of a great wine.

BRUNELLO DI MONTALCINO

Brunello di Montalcino, a wine produced in a small thirteenth-century hillside town south of Siena, is in the growing zone of Chianti Colli Senesi. This wine, stronger, fuller, and more fragrant than Chianti, is usually aged five to six years in cask, with a minimum of four years for the DOC wines, and two more years in bottle prior to sale. A Riserva has been aged at least five years before its sale. In addition to this, it should be given at least another ten years of bottle age before drinking. Some experts recommend decanting and breathing the wine for twenty-four hours before serving.

Signor Biondi-Santi is *the* most important grower, perhaps because the Biondi-Santi family is responsible for the reputation of this wine. Ancestor Ferruccio cultivated the Brunello grape in the nineteenth century; his first recorded vintage was in 1880, at his Cantina della Fattoría Il Greppo.

Other growers are Colombini, Costante, Franceschi, and Mastropaolo. The Brunello of only this last producer is generally available in this country, under his estate name, Poggia alle Mura.

The wine is made from 100% Brunello di Montalcino grapes, also known as Sangiovese Grosso. This variety is believed to have originated in Tuscany. It is grown on sunny hillsides at altitudes up to 2000 feet within the commune of Montalcino.

Rare and hard to find even in Tuscany, it is not generally available outside of Italy.

Its deep ruby color fades to garnet with age. Brunello has a huge body with a dry and warm concentrated flavor that is slightly tannic.

The wine is one of the longest-lived of all Italian wines.

Great vintages: 1945, 1955, 1961, 1964, 1970.

Very good vintages: 1946, 1947, 1950, 1951, 1952, 1957, 1958, 1959, 1966, 1967, 1971.

Drink with game and roasts.

VINO NOBILE DI MONTEPULCIANO

The commune of Montepulciano, which lies south of the Classico zone, is believed to be of Etruscan origin although no traces of that era now remain. In the sixth century the people of Chiusi, fleeing the barbarians, founded this town, perhaps on the site of a former settlement. The town, on the crest of a hill, was named Mons Politianus. This was eventually corrupted to Montepulciano.

The wine is produced from Prugnolo Gentile (Sangiovese Grosso) (50 to 70%), Canaiolo Nero (10 to 20%), Malvasia del Chianti, and Trebbiano Toscano grapes (10 to 20%), with up to 8% Pulcinculo also allowed. The vineyards are, at altitudes from 750 to 2000 feet, on the hilly terrain of the commune of Montepulciano in the province of Siena.

The history of this wine has been traced back to the thirteenth century. It enjoyed considerable popularity in the 1600s. Francesco Redi, in his seventeenth-century poem "Bacco in Toscana," used the phrase *d'ogni vino il re* (the king of all wines). This phrase has been picked up and used since to refer to Vino Nobile by the people of Montepulciano.

Vino Nobile di Montepulciano must be aged at least two years in wood and attain a minimum of 12% alcohol. If it has been aged for three years prior to sale, it may be labeled Riserva; and Riserva Speciale after four years of aging.

With age, its garnet color fades to a chestnut hue. This dry, slightly tannic wine has a deep scent of violets, and a slightly bitter finish which adds character.

Qualified wines are granted a neck label depicting a Sienese she-wolf by the local *consorzio*.

Great years: 1958, 1967, 1970, 1971.

Very good years: 1947, 1952, 1954, 1962, 1964, 1968.

The only Vino Nobile di Montepulciano generally available in the U.S. is that of Fassati.

Some notable producers:

Nobili Fratelli Luigi M. E. Leopoldo Bologna Buonsignori

Cantine Riunite N. H. Mario Contucci

Gr. Uff. Adamo Fanetti

Cantina Gattavecchi

This wine is a suitable accompaniment to red meat and game birds.

TUSCAN WHITES

The best Tuscan white wines are made from the Trebbiano and Malvasia grapes. Although Tuscany is now famous for its red Chianti, at one time the typical Tuscan wines were white. This situation prevailed up until the Renaissance, when red wine came to the fore.

Generally the Tuscan white wines are dry, fresh, and pleasant.

BRUT (SPUMANTE)

The house of Antinori, Villa Antinori, produces an excellent vintage *brut, méthode champenoise.* So does the house of Melini, labeled Ambassador Brut.

VIN SANTO

This amber-colored dessert wine is interesting on three scores: its name, its quality, and how it is made.

This is the best unfortified dessert wine from Italy that I have tasted to date, and the only one that I have had which can be called a great wine. A well-made Vin Santo has great balance, is velvety on the palate, and finishes with a pleasing dryness.

This wine, originally called *Vin Pretto*, was reputedly given its present name of Vin Santo in 1349. At a banquet in Florence given as part of an attempt to unite the eastern and western wings of the Catholic church, Vin Pretto was served at the finish of the repast. Upon tasting, Cardinal Bessarione, religious leader of the Greek Orthodox church and guest of honor, noting its similarity to a wine from his own country, exclaimed, "This is Xantos!"

The Florentines in attendance mistakenly thought that Bessarione had sanctified their wine by declaring it "*santo.*" The wine has been called Vin Santo ever since.

Another version of the story, which also credits Bessarione with the naming of this nectar at the banquet in Florence, relates that after tasting the wine the cardinal declared, "*Ma questo è un vino santo.*" (But this is a holy wine.)

Still another story explains that the wine is named to commemorate the time of its pressing—during Holy Week.

The method of production is interesting and unusual. After the harvest, the grapes are left to dry on frames or mats until about Easter time. At that time, the grapes are pressed and the juice is filtered into small barrels. These barrels are then stored in the attic. During the summer the attic gets very hot, and in the winter, very cold. In the summer the must ferments; in the winter it rests. Usually this process goes on for five years before the wine is filtered and bottled.

The result is a strong and velvety wine with a sweet flavor and a pleasingly dry finish. There is also a dry version of Vin Santo, but I've never encountered it.

The best Vin Santo is reputed to be from Val di Pesa in the Zona Classica south of Florence, and from the Casentino hills east of Florence.

The only Vin Santo available in the U.S. that I know of is the Vin Santo of Marchese Emilio Pucci.

CLASSICO CHIANTI

These generally range from about $3.50 to a bit under $5, but there are some good ones for less than $3, and a few approaching $8. Most Classicos above $4 are the Riservas, and most under $4.00 are not Riservas, but there are exceptions.

**Gabbiano Riserva	Bertolli
**Melini Riserva	Brolio Riserva
**Palazzo Al Bosco (Olivieri)	Buitoni
*Antinori	Buitoni Riserva
*Antinori Riserva	Cafaggio Riserva
*Antinori Santa Christina	Calcinaia
*Cappelli Riserva	Cappelli
*Melini	Cappelli La Quercia
*Nozzole Riserva	Capponi
*Pucci Castello di Cerreto Riserva	Carpinetto
	Casenuove
*Ruffino Riserva Ducale	Castello di Tizzano Riserva
*Ruffino Riserva Ducale gold label	Castel Vecchio
	Cecchi
*Soderi	Cecchi Cerna
*Straccalli Riserva	Coltibuono
*Verrazzano	Coltibuono Riserva
Albani Cantina del Pape	Corsini Riserva
Ancilli	Costa
Beccaro Riserva	Creazzo
Beccaro Vecchio	Forna

Gancia
Grevepesa
Machiavelli
Melzzano (Falcani)
Mirafiore
Mirafiore Riserva del Conte
Montepaldi (M. Corsina)

Nuove
Pagni
Rencine Riserva
Selve
Serristori St. Andrea
Suali
Vecchiomaggio

CHIANTI

Most of these wines are in the almost-$2-to-under-$3 range. A few are about $3.50, a couple approach $5.

*Capezzana Riserva
*Giannozzi Riserva
*Serristori (*putto*)
Barbero Mezzano
Bardi
Barsottini
Beccaro
Bertolli
Bertolli Bambino
Bigi
Borghini
Bruni
Capezzano Carmignano
Cavalier
Certaldo Castel
Certaldo Opici
Certaldo Valbella
Conte Vecchio
Cusona
Dellavalle Riserva

Fassati Riserva
Fassati Valdoro
Felini
Forra
Franchi
Frescobaldi
Frescobaldi Nippozzano
Frescobaldi Riserva
Gherzi
Giannozzi
Grasiosi
Magni
Marcaverde
Melini
Mirafiore
Montorsello La Querce
Perlino
Pietrini
Pillo
Pucci Granaiolo

Raspollini
Ricasoli
Rosito
Ruffino
Spada

Torre
Tytell
Victori
Vigna

TUSCAN WHITES

Generally about $2.50 to $3.50; a few are over $4, a few less than $2.50.

*Melini Lacrima d'Arno
*Ruffino Tuscan
Antinori Bianco della Costa Toscana
Antinori Bianco Secco
Brolio
Bruni Vernaccia
Capezzano
Cappelli La Quercia
Cappelli Vino Bianco
Cusona
Frescobaldi Pomino
Machiavelli Serristori
Marca Verdi
Mirafiore
Montepaldi
Pasolini Montepetri
Pucci Granaiolo Secco
Verrazzano

TUSCAN ROSES

These wines range from approximately $2.50 to about $3.50, although there are exceptions.

* Melini Rose Reale
Antinori Rose di Bolgheri
Bertolli Vinrosa
Bigi Flamenco
Brolio
Cappelli Selvanella
Pucci
Ruffino Rosatello (from Sangiovese
   grapes)
Verrazzano

TUSCAN REDS

These usually retail in the $2.50-to-$3.50 range.

Bertoli Bambino
Bonizio
Frescobaldi Pomino
Grifoni
Ruffino del Magnifico

TUSCAN SPUMANTE

Around $8.

Marchese Antinori Nature Brut

VIN SANTO

This wine goes for about $4.

**Pucci Fattoria di Granaiolo

VINO NOBILE DI MONTEPULCIANO

This wine sells for approximately $4.

*Fassati *(older vintages)*
Fassati *(younger vintages)*

BRUNELLO DI MONTALCINO

This one is in the $7 range.

Poggia alle Mura

UMBRIA

Umbria is a region of green, winding valleys, lakes, river basins, poplar trees, and hills crowned with medieval cities. The pastures of the Clitumnus Valley were famous in ancient times. This is the only region bordered by Italy on all sides.

ORVIETO

The only well-known wine from this region is Orvieto. This wine, known since the fifteenth century, is from the medieval town of that name. Two versions are produced: *abboccato* and *secco*.

Orvieto is frequently sold, like many of the *governo* Chiantis, in straw-covered flasks. These are more squat than the Chianti *fiaschi*, however, and are called *pulcianelle*.

The *vino secco*, with a slight bitter touch at the end, is between 12 and 14% alcohol; while the *abboccato*, at 11 to 13%, is not as strong. The *abboccato* has more character than the *secco*.

The *abboccato* is produced from grapes affected with *muffa nobile* (noble rot). The major difference between these wines and the Sauternes of France or the great Auslesen of Germany is that these grapes are picked just as they begin to be affected by the mold rather than being left on the vine until the process is complete, as in those countries. The resultant wine is therefore not as sweet.

After the harvest, the grapes are placed in open trays to

114

continue rotting in the caves nearby. The town of Orvieto rises from a cliff which is honeycombed with caves. In many respects, the wine and the caves of Orvieto remind one of the wine and caves of Vouvray and Saumur in the Loire Valley of France.

Orvieto is protected by the Consorzio per la Difesa del Vino Tipico di Orvieto. The following grape varieties are used: Trebbiano Toscano (Procanico [50 to 65%]), Verdello (15 to 25%), and Malvasia, Grechetto, and Drupeggio (20 to 30%, with no more than 20% of that from the Malvasia).

Drink either version well chilled with seafood or fresh-water fish. The *abboccato* is a good accompaniment to fowl. The *secco* makes a good apéritif.

TORGIANO

DOC allows this wine to be either red or white. The grapes must be grown around the commune of Torgiano; this encompasses the area from Assisi (famous as the town of St. Francis) to Perugia, and includes vineyards on the banks of the Tiber and Chiascio Rivers.

The village is named for the imposing Tower of Janus (*Torre di Giano*) which stands watch over the town. This tower was named for the Roman god who was the guardian of the grape.

The red wine must be from 50 to 70% Sangiovese, 15 to 30% Canaiolo, 10% Trebbiano Toscano, and up to 10% Ciliegiolo or Montepulciano. DOC specifies at least 12% alcohol for this rich, fruity wine.

Its color is a brilliant ruby red, its aroma is intensely vinous, and it finishes with a pleasing dryness. At a recent blind tasting, the Lungarotti Rubesco Torgiano stood out as a very impressive bottle of wine. It has an extraordinary richness.

The Torgiano Bianco is a straw-colored fruity wine. It must

be made from 50 to 70% Trebbiano Toscano, 15 to 30% Grechetto, and up to 15% Malvasia Toscana, Malvasia di Candia, or Verdello. DOC specifies at least 11.5% alcoholic content.

Serve the red with veal or fowl, although it *will* stand up to a steak. The white goes well with cold cuts, and is also recommended by some with fish chowder. (I would prefer a dry Marsala with this latter dish myself.)

ORVIETO

Generally around $2.50 to $3.50; one or two sell for less.

*Antinori Abboccato Castellola Scala
*Melini Secco
*Ruffino Abboccato
 Bigi Abboccato
 Borghini
 Cappelli Secco
 Carpineto Secco
 Cella
 Gancia
 Melini Abboccato
 Mirafiore
 Montresor Abboccato
 Montresor Secco
 Perlino
 Pertrurbani Abboccato
 Pertrurbani Secco
 Ruffino Secco
 Vaselli Secco

TORGIANO

Most of these are less than $3; one of them, the Riserva, is over $4.

**Lungarotti Rubesco
*Lungarotti Rubesco Riserva
Lungarotti Buffaloro
Lungarotti Castel Grifone
Lungarotti Rosciano
Lungarotti Torre di Giano
Lungarotti Vin Santo

OTHERS

These wines are in the $2.50 to $3.50 range.

Mirafiore Rose
Vaselli Rose

MARCHE

Marche, with a smooth coastline on the Adriatic Sea to the east, is furrowed by a series of deep narrow valleys. This region, noted for its cereals, produces a white wine considered by some to be almost on a par with Soave—Verdicchio dei Castelli di Jesi.

VERDICCHIO DEI CASTELLI DI JESI

This wine must be made from the Verdicchio grape and attain no less than 11.5% alcohol under the DOC regulation. A Classico designation is allowed for the wines produced in the Zona Antica, the classical zone for this wine.

This Verdicchio is pale straw in color, has a subtle aroma, and a dry, fruity flavor with a slightly bitter aftertaste.

The best Verdicchios are made by the *governo* system of introducing a secondary fermentation by the addition of fresh juice to the must. Consequently these wines are best when young, within a year or two of the vintage. Drink them with fish or cold white meats.

VERDICCHIO DI MATELICA

Another one, Verdicchio di Matelica, although not quite as good as the Castelli di Jesi, is still a good bottle of wine. This straw-colored wine is made from no less than 80% Verdicchio grapes with the addition of up to 20% Trebbiano Bianco and Malvasia Toscana. This wine must be at least 12% alcohol to meet the DOC requirement.

It goes with the same food as the Verdicchio dei Castelli di Jesi.

ROSSO PICENO

Rosso Piceno is the best red wine of the Marche. It is also the region's oldest known wine, having been traced back to Hannibal and the Greek colonists.

The vines are planted on the hills of Ascoli Piceno, Ancona, and Macerata. This wine has the greatest production of any of the wines of the Marche. It is made from a minimum of 60% Sangiovese and a maximum of 40% Montepulciano grapes.

DOC requires that this light, clear, ruby-colored wine be at least 11.5% alcohol. A Superiore designation on the label is allowed to wines produced from grapes grown in fourteen communes in the province of Ascoli Piceno, if the alcoholic content is no less than 12% and the wine has been aged at least one year prior to its sale.

Serve with white meats and poultry, slightly chilled.

ROSSO CONERO

Rosso Conero is from Montepulciano (no less than 85%) and Sangiovese (no more than 15%) grapes grown on the Conero hills of seven communes in the Ancona province. The DOC regulation specifies a minimum of 11.5% alcohol.

This ruby-colored, dry, fruity wine is light and pleasant. It also goes well with white meats.

The wine is sometimes labeled Montepulciano del Conero.

VERDICCHIO

Most are about $3; a few are closer to $4.

*Fazi Battaglia Titulus (di Jesi)
Agrario Provinciale (di Jesi)
Aurora (di Jesi)
Beccaro
Bianchi
Bianci
Buitoni
Catellucci (di Jesi)
Cella (di Jesi)
Cupramontana (di Jesi)
Cupranectar (di Jesi)
Opici
Pavan
Tombolini (di Jesi)
Torelli
Torri
Umani Ronchi (di Jesi)

ROSSO PICENO

Under $3.

**Cupramontana
Villa di Boccabianca

ROSSO CONERO

Under $3.

Buitoni
Umani Ronchi

OTHERS

Prices range between $2.50 and $4.

**Solazzi Bianchello del Metauro
Aurora Rosato

Fazi Battaglia Collameno Rose
Fazi Battaglia Rutilus Red
Gian Paolo Brut Spumante
Umani Ronchi Rosato

ABRUZZO AND MOLISE

Abruzzo, a region of huge chalk mountains and narrow gorges, with a harsh, windy climate, is the major wool-producing area of the country. Here are the Gran Sasso and Maiella massifs, meadows and rich plantations, almond trees, olive groves, and vineyards. Grapes are planted on the sunny side of the hills overlooking the Adriatic Sea to the east. L'Aquila (the eagle) is the capital of this agricultural region.

TREBBIANO D'ABRUZZO

This golden-colored, dry wine is made from grapes of the same name (with the addition of no more than 15% of Malvasia Toscana, Coccocciola, and Passerina allowed). It must contain 12% alcohol.

Oftentimes common and sharp, it can be pleasant and refreshing. Trebbiano d'Abruzzo goes well with fish and shellfish. Especially recommended with fish soup *alla tiella*.

MONTEPULCIANO D'ABRUZZO

This light red wine is made from Montepulciano grapes (with the addition of no more than 15% Sangiovese allowed) grown on the eastern slopes of the Apennines. It is a rather ordinary wine. Its ruby color fades to garnet with age. It has a cherrylike aroma and a slight sweetness on the palate. DOC requires at least 12% alcohol.

122

If aged for two years in wood, it can be labeled Vecchio.
Serve with white meat and fowl.

A cherry-colored rose, Cerasuolo, from Malvasia grapes, is also produced.

MOLISE

Molise, a mountainous area of dark valleys and wild forests, produces no wine currently imported into the United States.

WINES OF ABRUZZO

Under $3.

**Casal Thaulero Montepulciano d'Abruzzo
Casal Thaulero Trebbiano d'Abruzzo
de Sanctis Montepulciano d'Abruzzo

LAZIO

Lazio is located in the western central part of Italy, between the Tyrrhenian Sea and the Apennines. This region was the cradle of Roman civilization, and numerous ruins from that era may be seen throughout the area. The regional capital is Rome.

Vines grow in the hills around Rome, the Castelli Romani (Roman castles), and the Lake Bolsena area. The soil of both of these areas is volcanic. The best wines of this region are white.

EST! EST!! EST!!! DI MONTEFIASCONE

Est! Est!! Est!!! di Montefiascone, a light, dry or semi-sweet white wine made from 65% Trebbiano (Procanico), 15% Rossetto (Trebbiano Giallo), and 20% Malvasia Toscana grapes is grown near Montefiascone, close to the shores of Lake Bolsena, north of Rome. This wine, from the province of Viterbo, was the second Italian wine to be awarded a DOC (1966). The following communes are entitled to this name—Bolsena, Capodimonte, Gradoli, Grotte di Castro, Marta, Montefiascone, and San Lorenzo Nuovo.

The most interesting thing about this wine is how it got its name: In 1110, Bishop Johann Fugger of Augsburg, on his way to the coronation of Henry V in Rome, sent Martin, his major domo, on ahead to check out the wines at the inns along the way. His instructions were to mark the door of any inn *Est* ("it is," short for *vinum bonum est*) if the wine was good. When Martin got to Montefiascone—so the story goes—he found the

124

wine so good that he wrote "Est! Est!! Est!!!" on the tavern door. Bishop Fugger duly stopped at the inn and was so impressed that he took up residence in the town. The story does not tell whether he ever got to Rome, but we do know that the good bishop died and was buried in Montefiascone. If you are interested, a tombstone may be seen in the church of San Flaviano with the inscription:

Est. Est. Propter Nimium (Est. Est. Because of too much
Est Hic Jo. Defuk Dominus Est. here Jo. Defuk, my master
Meus Mortus Est is dead.)

It seems that the bishop was so taken by the town producing the charming wine that when he became a citizen, he Italianized his German name also.

According to the story, the bishop willed that every year on the anniversary of his death, a barrel of Est! Est!! Est!!! should be poured over his grave. This was the condition set forth by the good bishop when he left his earthly possessions to the small town. Cardinal Barberigo, Bishop of Montefiascone, stopped this practice, however, arguing that this was a terrible waste of their delightful wine. He ordered it to be sent to the local seminary to be enjoyed by the priests instead, in memory of their benefactor.

Originally Est! Est!! Est!!! was a Moscatello wine; today it is a Trebbiano. This wine is a pale-straw color with a vinous nose and a dry flavor. Drink it with fish, especially pike and eels.

FRASCATI

The region's most famous wine, Frascati, is from the Castelli Romani area, south and west of Rome. This wine is made from Malvasia Bianca di Candia, Malvasia del Lazio (Puntinata), Greco (Trebbiano Giallo), Trebbiano Toscano, and no more than 10% of Bellone and Bonvino grapes grown in volcanic soil in or near the communes of Frascati, Grottaferrata, and Colonna Roma.

This light, straw-colored wine comes in three types: *secco* or *asciutto, amabile,* and *cannellino* or *dolce.* The *secco* retains up to 1% of unfermented sugar; the *amabile,* from 1 to 3%; and the *cannellino,* from 3 to 6%. Regardless of the sweetness, Frascati has a fragrant aroma and a light, clear, golden color.

Normally 11.5% alcohol, to be labeled Superiore, Frascati must be at least 12%. A *spumante* version can also be found.

Due to the humidity, the plants of this region are afflicted with *pourriture gris* (gray rot). This disease causes the grapes to lose liquid, tannin, and sugar. In addition, the grapes pick up undesirable bacteria. It is similar to the *pourriture noble,* which is a desirable mold affecting the great Sauternes and the Rieslings of Germany, and resulting in a golden, sweet nectar. The dividing line between the noble rot and the gray rot is very fine and visually difficult to distinguish.

Generally, the rot of Frascati is of the gray variety, and is undesirable. To eliminate it, the grapes are given a light pressing and the skins are quickly discarded. After a dose of sulfur and a flash pasturization, the wine is left to rest.

This wine is recommended with pasta; the *secco* also with artichokes *alla romana.* The *cannellino* is especially good with gnocchi. Of the three versions, the sweet is considered to be the best.

CASTELLI ROMANI

The Castelli Romani wines are grown in a fifty-square-mile area (delimited by law in 1933) in the Alban hills southeast of Rome. Most of them are white—*secco, amabile,* or *dolce.* The latter two versions, described as mellow, are the most common both here and in Italy.

The *dolce* wines are produced from late-picked grapes afflicted with *pourriture gris*, gray rot. The same problem exists with these other Castelli Romani wines as with Frascati (see above). Because the weather is cold when the grapes are picked and crushed, the fermentation is slow.

The white wines are from Bellone, Malvasia di Candia, Malvasia del Lazio, Bonvino and Trebbiano Toscano grapes. Red and rose wines are also made.

The Castelli Romani wines include:

Colli Albani (see description)
Colli Lanuvini (see description)
Colonna (a white wine of 11.5% alcohol)
Cori (a red of 11.5% alcohol and a white of 11%)
Frascati (see description)
Marino (see description)
Montecompatri (a white wine of 11.5% alcohol)
Velletri (see description)
Zagarolo (a white wine of 11.5% alcohol)

COLLI ALBANI

Colli Albani is made from Malvasia Rossa (or Malvasia Bianca di Candia) (up to 60%), Trebbiano Toscano (25 to 50%), Bonvino and Cacchione (up to 10%), and Malvasia del Lazio (Puntinata [15 to 45%]) grapes grown in the communes of Albano, Ariccia and part of Roma, Castelgandolfo and Pomezia. It is straw-yellow in color with a delicate nose and a dry flavor which has a slight sweetness. It contains 11.5% alcohol.

It is a good accompaniment to pasta dishes and fresh-water fish.

COLLI LANUVINI

This straw-colored wine from the communes of Genzano and Lanuvio may be dry or semisweet. It is a full-bodied wine of no less than 11.5% alcohol and goes well with pasta and fish, although it is highly recommended with asparagus dishes.

Colli Lanuvini must be from no more than 70% Malvasia di Candia, and no less than 30% Trebbiano Toscano grapes. Up to 10% Bellone and Bonvino may be added.

MARINO

Marino is made from Malvasia, Trebbiano, and Puntinata grapes grown along the northern shores of Lake Albino. It is a pale-colored, mellow wine without much character, but its price makes it one of the best buys of the region. Serve well chilled—almost frozen.

This wine is supposed to go well with onion soup.

VELLETRI

Velletri is similar to Frascati, but lighter in color, body, and flavor. This wine ends with a slight bitterness. They say that the red has more character, but it is unavailable in this country. The white is highly recommended with artichoke dishes, especially *carciofi alla matticella* (artichokes marinated in oil and cooked on vine twig embers).

FRASCATI

Normally priced between about $2 and $3.50.

**de Sanctis
*Fontana Candida (Superiore)
*Marino
*Valle Vermiglia
Azienda Vinicole Vigneti SS. Apostoli
Beccaro
Castelli Romani
Cella
Campo-Romano
Commandini
Fontana di Trevi
Magistri
Marino (Superiore)
Pavan
De Sanctis (Superiore)
Torri

VELLETRI

About $3.

Pavan

MARINO

About $3.

Cantina Sociale di Marino

COLLI ALBANI

Prices are about $3.

Barberini (white)
Cantina Sociale Colli Albani (white)

COLLI LANUVINI

About $3.

San Gennaro (dry white)

CASTELLI ROMANI

Prices range from about $2 to about $3.

Azienda Vinicole Vigneti SS. Apostoli red
Barberini Red
Barberini Rose
Cantina Sociale Colli Albani Red
Cantina Sociale Colli Albani Rose
Casallini Roman Red
Castelli Romani Red
Cella Red
Commandini Vino Rosso
Fontana di Trevi Red
Marino Rosato
Marino Rubino
Valle Vermiglia Red

EST! EST!! EST!!!

In the $3.50 range.

Antinori

SOUTHERN ITALY
AND THE ISLANDS

CAMPANIA

This densely populated region, with Naples as its capital, is an area of fertile volcanic plains, Roman ruins—Pompeii and Herculaneum—the resort islands of Capri and Ischia in the Bay of Naples, and what might well be the most spectacular scenery in Europe—the Amalfi coast. This dramatic coastline runs from Sorrento to Salerno, offering breathtaking views of sheer cliffs, covered with colorful flowers and lush greenery, which in some places rise straight up from the sea.

The volcanic soil of Campania yields hemp, corn, olives, and cereals, as well as a lot of the coarse blending wine produced here. Vines can be seen here clinging to the poplar trees.

RAVELLO

Ravello Bianco, Rosato, and Rosso are produced in the Sorrento Peninsula west of Salerno. The *Rosato* has a touch of sweetness that many find pleasant, but the *Bianco* is the best of the three. Ravello Bianco is a pale-straw-colored wine with a dry flavor. (I still retain a fondness for the Caruso Ravello Bianco as this was my introduction to Italian wine some fifteen years ago.) The Ravello Rosato is a mellow rosé with a sweet touch. The Ravello Rosso is ruby-red in color with a sweet aftertaste. It goes well with pork, veal, or fowl.

133

LACRIMA CHRISTI

Lacrima Christi (tear of Christ) is from vines grown on the seaward side of Mount Vesuvius, although some plants grown on the eastern side are also used.

There is an interesting story behind the name of this wine: According to the legend, Lucifer, as he was thrown out of heaven, grasped a piece of heaven which fell down with him. This was the origin of the Bay of Naples, which is indeed a beautiful piece of countryside. Later, when Christ saw the sinning that was going on down there, he shed a tear which fell on the vineyards around Mount Vesuvius, and the wines have been richer and better ever since. (The people are hoping to be punished like that again!)

Lacrima Christi is made from Coda di Volpe, Greco di Torre, and Biancolella grapes grown on the southern slopes of Mount Vesuvius. It is a pale-straw-colored dry wine with a flowery scent. It has a delicate flavor and a slight sweetness. Although a red and a rosé are bottled by this name, they are not true Lacrima Christis. The Rosso goes with pork and veal dishes, while the Bianco is a fitting accompaniment to fish.

In the Bay of Naples, where Ulysses on his Odyssey barely escaped from the sirens, lie the islands of Capri, Procida, and Ischia. The wines of Capri are rarely seen outside of the island itself, but those of Ischia can be found in the United States.

ISCHIA ROSSO

Ischia Rosso is made from 50% Guarnaccia, 40% Per' 'e Palummo (Piedirosso), and 10% Barbera grapes. This deep-ruby wine has a vinous nose, and a dry, tannic touch. It contains 11.5% alcohol. This wine, along with the Ischia Bianco, was the third wine to be granted a DOC, immediately after Vernaccia di San Gimignano and Est! Est!! Est!!! di Montefiascone. Serve the Rosso with meat stews.

ISCHIA BIANCO

The Bianco is made from 65% Forastera, 20% Biancolella, and no more than 15% of other varieties. Is is straw in color with a delicate, vinous nose and a dry flavor. It contains 11% alcohol. Serve with fish. If the label reads Superiore, the Bianco must be at least 11.5% alcohol and be made from 50% Forastera, 40% Biancolella, and 10% San Lunardo grapes.

BIANCOLELLA

Biancolella is a straw-colored wine made from the grapes of the same name. It has a delicate, aromatic nose and a dry flavor that hints of almonds. Its alcoholic content is 12%. Serve cold with seafood or mild cheeses. Salmon goes well with this wine.

PER' 'E PALUMMO

Per' 'e Palummo, from grapes of the same name, is a ruby-colored, vinous wine that is dry and velvety on the palate. Its 12% alcoholic content requires a robust piece of meat, such as game or a red-meat roast. It also goes well with strong cheeses. This wine requires a minimum of two hours of air prior to serving in order to open up and soften.

RAVELLO

Available for about $4.

*Caruso Bianco
Caruso Rosato
Caruso Rosso

LACRIMA CHRISTI

Between $3 and $4.

*Scala White
Perrazzo White
Scala Red

ISCHIAN WINES

From about $2.50 to approximately $4.

*D'Ambra Bianco
*Perrazzo Rosso
D'Ambra Biancolla
D'Ambra Per' 'e Palummo
D'Ambra Rosso
Perrazzo Bianco
Perrazzo Bianco Superiore

OTHERS

About $3 to $4.

Perrazzo Don Alfonzo Bianco
Perrazzo Don Alfonzo Rosado
Perrazzo Don Alfonzo Rosso

APULIA

Apulia, the heel of Italy, is easily the largest wine-producing region, in volume, of the country. Most of this highly alcoholic wine is used for blending—the whites for Vermouth, the reds to add strength and body to the thinner wines of the north.

The mild winters here give way to hot summers. The sunny climate and heavy soil result in grapes with high sugar content which yield wines of high alcoholic content.

CASTEL DEL MONTE

Castel del Monte, between Barletta and the region's capital, Bari, has been awarded a DOC which applies to its Rosso, Rosato, and Bianco wines.

The Rosso is produced from Bombino Nero grapes with a little Montepulciano allowed. These vines grow in stony soil on the hills around the communes of Andria, Bisceglie, and Trani. This ruby-colored wine takes on an orange hue with age. It is normally aged for three years prior to sale, one in cask, and reaches 12.5% alcohol.

The wine will last a decade or more. When it is young, less than six years old, it should be given a minimum of two hours of air prior to being served. Its dry, tannic flavor goes well with red-meat roasts or steaks.

Rivera produces a Fascia Rossa which is aged for a minimum of two years in cask.

The Rivera vines, producing Rosso, Rosato, and Bianco

wines, grow from 1000 to 1500 feet above sea level. This helps prevent the fruit from ripening too early. Normally the grapes are harvested in August. Both of these factors combine to result in reduced sugar, and higher acidity—hence, lower alcohol and better balance.

A light ruby-pink Rosato, that is said to have an aroma of ripe fruit, is made from the same grapes as the Rosso. It is the most renowned of the Castel del Monte wines.

The Bianco is produced from Panpanuto, Bombino Bianco, and Trebbiano grapes. It is a dry wine that should be served very cold and is excellent with hors d'oeuvre.

SAN STEFANO

San Stefano, from the province of Foggia, was granted a DOC in 1968. The Rosso must be from at least 70% Montepulciano d'Abruzzo, and no more than 30% Sangiovese grapes. This ruby-colored wine contains at least 11.5% alcohol. It is pleasantly dry and rich on the palate and goes well with rich tomato sauces or steaks. This wine ages quite well. One of the most noted producers is Dr. Cirilio Farrusi, who bottles his San Stefano Rosso as Torre Quarto. With age, this wine takes on a garnet hue.

SAN SEVERO

DOC allows the use of this name for white, red, and rosé wines, when they are produced from grapes grown within eight specified communes, including San Severo, in the province of Foggia.

Originally, the name San Severo was used to refer to white wine only, while the reds from the same area were called San Stefano.

The whites must be made from 40 to 60% Bombino Bianco

grapes, 40 to 60% Trebbiano Toscano, and no more than 20% Malvasia del Chianti and Verdea. This pale-straw-colored wine has a vinous scent and a dry flavor. It must attain at least 11% alcohol. DOC also allows this wine to be made *spumante*, although it is not often done.

Much of the white wine from the Foggia plain is exported to be used in Vermouth. The better wines are sold with the San Severo *denominazione*.

The Rosso and the Rosato must be from no less than 70% Montepulciano d'Abruzzo, and no more than 30% Sangiovese; 100% of the former is therefore allowed. The ruby-colored red or the rather transparent ruby-colored rose must attain a minimum of 11.5% alcohol. The aroma is vinous, and the flavor dry.

CASTEL DEL MONTE

In the $2.50 to $3.50 range.

**Rivera Castel del Monte Rosso
*Rivera Castel del Monte Bianco
Rivera Castel del Monte Rose

SAN STEFANO

Approximately $3.50.

**Cirillo-Farrusi Torre Quarto

SAN SEVERO

In the $3 to $4 range.

*Casteldrione d'Alfonso del Sordo
*Montero d'Alfonso del Sordo
Bianco d'Alfonso del Sordo
Rosato d'Alfonso del Sordo

BASILICATA

Basilicata is a wild and rocky land of citrus groves, olive trees, chestnut forests, and vineyards. None of its wines make it to the United States. Most are used for blending, or are shipped to northern Italy for Vermouth. The best wines come from the foot and lower slopes of the extinct volcano Vulture.

AGLIANICO DEL VULTURE

Aglianico del Vulture is one of the best wines of Italy. The vines are planted in the volcanic soil of the lower slopes of Mount Vulture. It is reputed that this garnet-colored wine will live for a long time and, indeed, requires many years in the bottle in order to smooth out. With sufficient age, it becomes austere and smooth.

After two years in wood and one more in bottle, the wine may be labeled Vecchio. If aged for two additional years (in bottle) prior to its sale, it may be labeled Riserva.

With proper age, this rich, red, dry, tannic wine goes well with highly flavored dishes, including those that are hot. It is especially recommended with lamb stew, *cutturiddu.*

Unfortunately, it is not currently available in the United States.

CALABRIA

Calabria, the sunny toe of Italy, is rugged and mountainous. This region, noted for its agricultural output, is responsible for much of the blending wines of Italy. The coarse whites are used for Vermouth while the heavy reds are added to some of the thinner wines of northern Italy or shipped to France for the same purpose.

CIRÒ

Cirò is a big, robust wine that is available as a Rosso, Rosato, and Bianco. The Rosso is from 90% Gaglioppo (Magliocco) and Piedilungo (Greco Bianco) grapes grown north of Crotone, near the commune of Cirò. The Bianco, from Greco Bianco grapes grown in the same region, has a distinctive aroma and a dry taste.

After long aging, the ruby color of the Cirò Rosso takes on an orange hue. It has an intense aroma and a slight sweetness on the palate. Cirò is known for its exceptional longevity and its high alcoholic content. DOC requires at least 13.5% alcohol, but 14 to 15% is not uncommon; in some years the level reaches 17%.

There is a classical zone—Cirò and Cirò Marina. If aged three years in wood the wine may be labeled Riserva.

Great year: 1968.

Very good years: 1960, 1961, 1964.

This big wine is a suitable accompaniment to game, beef, and spicy dishes, also strong cheeses.

141

CIRÒ

These are available from about $3 to about $4.

**Caruso Cirò Classico
*Caruso Rose del Golfo
Caruso Bianco del Golfo
Caruso Gaglioppo
Catanzaro Bianco
Catanzaro Cirò Classico
Catanzaro Rosato
Cirovin Cirò Bianco
Cirovin Cirò Rosato
Cirovin Cirò Rosso Classico
Cirovin Cirò Rosso Classico Riserva
Ippolito Cirò Classico
Librandi Cirò Bianco
Librandi Cirò Rosato
Librandi Cirò Rosso Classico
Librandi Cirò Rosso Classico Riserva

SICILY

Sicily, the largest island in the Mediterranean, with an area of over 10,000 square miles, is rugged and mountainous; one fourth of its total area is covered by mountains, some two thirds of the island is over 900 feet above sea level. The most impressive physical feature of this sun-parched, triangular island is Mount Etna, Europe's largest active volcano. This forbidding 11,000-foot volcano is visible for a distance of 150 miles, and looms in marked contrast to the wheat fields, citrus groves, and plains dotted with olive, almond, and walnut trees, date palms, fig and pomegranate bushes, which grow profusely in the fertile volcanic soil.

The history of viticulture in Sicily is ancient: the Greeks, in the eighth century B.C., are known to have produced wine there.

Due to the hot climate, most of the wine is coarse and heavy and is shipped north for blending. Many of the following wines are not available in the United States at this time, but because of current interest in the American market on the part of the Sicilian producers, there is a good chance that many of the better wines will be imported in the coming months. Consequently, I am including them here. Many of the Sicilian wines represent an excellent value in today's market.

ALCAMO

Alcamo, or Bianco Alcamo, is named for the town of Alcamo near the Castellamare Gulf where it is produced. This dry white wine has been awarded a DOC, which requires 11.5% alcohol. Alcamo is made from Catarratto Lucido grapes (other varieties, no more than 20%, are allowed). It is usually shipped north to be used for Vermouth as it generally lacks acidity and is therefore flabby.

A local variety, named Segesta for the Roman city in its growing area, is protected by a *consorzio*. This wine is currently imported into the United States, as is a Segesta Red. Both are worthwhile wines.

CERASUOLO

Cerasuolo, a cherry-colored rosé, is produced in the communes of Floridia, Isola, and Vittoria, in the southeastern corner of Sicily. This full-bodied wine has an herby scent and should go well with rich dishes. It is made from a mixture of black (red) and white grapes: Albanello, Calabrese, Frappato, and Grossonero.

The Cerasuolo di Vittoria is reputed to be the best, and the di Floridia the heaviest. They say this latter is better for blending than for drinking.

Some say this wine is best when young; others, that it will age for up to thirty years, when its color fades to an ash white. Perhaps the discrepancy can be accounted for by differences among the communes.

The wine from Vittoria, Cerasuolo di Vittoria, has been granted a DOC. This Cerasuolo is reputed to be the best, as mentioned. The grapes used in its production are Calabrese (up to 60%) and Frappato (not less than 40%). It must attain 13% alcohol.

CORVO

Corvo, near Palermo, lends its name to a dry red wine made from Perricone and Catanese grapes, as well as a white wine from Cataratto and Inzolia grapes. Colomba Platino is the classic zone for this latter wine.

Look for Duca di Salaparuta, which includes a Bianco, Rosso, Rosso Riserva, Colomba Platino, Stravecchio, and a liqueur named Corvo Ala.

According to Cyril Ray the name Corvo (Italian for crow) comes from a complicated legend involving a hermit, a noisy raven, a stick given the hermit by the sympathetic populace to drive the bird away, and the vine which sprang from the stick.

ETNA

Etna Bianco, Rosso, and Rosato are produced from grapes grown on the lower and middle slopes of Mount Etna, at an altitude of up to 3500 feet. The *denominazione* (DOC) covers twenty communes in the province of Catania in the immediate vicinity of Mount Etna.

This wine was first mentioned by Homer; it was the wine used by Ulysses to disarm the Cyclops Polyphemus by getting him drunk so that Ulysses could blind him. (He succeeded.)

DOC requires the Bianco to be made from a minimum of 60% Carricante, up to 40% Catarratto Bianco grapes, allowing no more than 15% of other varieties (Inzolia, Minnella, and Trebbiano). Etna Bianco must be at least 11% alcohol.

This straw-colored wine has a greenish tint, an intense aroma, and a dry flavor. Sometimes it is *frizzante*.

If the wine is from grapes grown in the commune of Milo, in a proportion of no less than 80% Carricante, and contains at least 12% alcohol, it may be labeled Superiore. This wine has a delicate, fruity nose and a dry, pleasing flavor. Serve with fish or shellfish.

Etna Rosso and Etna Rosato must be from no less than 80% Nerello Mascalese grapes and no more than 20% Nerello Mantella. Other varieties, up to 10%, are allowed. The ruby-colored red becomes garnet with age. It is light, dry, and astringent with a hint of bitterness at the end. It is aged for three years in cask prior to sale. Its minimum alcoholic content is 12.5%. The dark-colored rosé has similar characteristics. Serve with poultry; especially recommended with *melanzane* (eggplant) *alla siciliana.*

Most of these wines are sent north for blending or are exported (to Germany) to be used for brandy or Vermouth.

Better reds come from Biancavilla, Ciclopi, Ragalma, and Ragabo. Also worth searching for are Linguaglossa and Sant'Alfio.

The best wines come from the middle slopes, at an approximate altitude of 2000 feet—Etnei di Mezza Montagna.

Great Vintage: 1962.

Very good vintages: 1968, 1967, 1965, 1964, 1961, 1960.

FARO

Faro, one of the better Sicilian reds, is from Nerello Cappuccio, Nerello Mascalese, and Nocera grapes grown on the hills above the Messina straits in the northeastern corner of the island. This ruby-colored wine has a delicate nose and a dry flavor. For a wine produced in this hot southern climate, it is light in body. Prior to its sale, it is aged for two years in cask.

Spinasanta is a highly esteemed producer who also bottles an Etna Vecchio.

MALVASIA DI LIPARI

Malvasia di Lipari, sweet and golden-colored, is one of the best dessert wines of Sicily. This wine is made from Malvasia grapes grown on the Lipari Islands, also called the Aeolian Group, north of Messina. Lipari is the major town on the island of the same name. Most of the wine, however, comes from the other islands, chiefly Salina and Stromboli.

To make this lusciously rich wine, Malvasia grapes are pressed when they are nearly dried. The alcoholic content is increased (to 16%) and the fermentation arrested by the addition of neutral spirits. The wine is then left to age in cask for three years. Most of it is bottled in Messina or Naples.

Spinasanta is a respected producer who also bottles the dessert wines Mamertino and Moscato Passito di Pantelleria (see below).

MOSCATO

There are many Moscatos produced in Sicily. They are usually qualified by a place name, such as:

di Chiaramonte
di Comiso
di Noto
di Pantelleria
di Segesta
di Siracusa
di Vittoria
lo Zucco

They are all amber-colored, richly sweet dessert wines made from semidried Moscato grapes.

The Moscato lo Zucco is also known as Goccia d'Oro.

The Moscato di Siracusa, considered to be the best, has an older historical reference than any other wine: King Pollius, according to the history, brought the Moscato vines to Syracuse from Thrace in the seventh century B.C.

Moscato di Pantelleria is actually made from Zibibbo (Moscatellone), a variety of Moscato grown on the island of Pantelleria southwest of Sicily. A Moscato Passito di Pantelleria is also made on this island.

REGALEALI

Regaleali, from the estate of Count Tasca d'Almerita in the hills between Palermo and Caltanisetta, is a highly esteemed wine. Since 1830, Count Tasca and his family have imposed strict supervision over the production of these wines.

The red and rosé are from Nero d'Avola and Nerello Mascalese grapes grown at an altitude of 1500 feet. The white is from Catarratto and Inzolia vines grown at the same high altitude.

At a recent tasting of Italian wines, the Regaleali red showed very well.

VALLEDOLMO AND VALLELUNGA

Valledolmo, near Palermo, and Vallelunga, in the center of the island, lend their names to some very similar wines, both in red and white. These wines are produced from the same grapes in both places. The white, from Catarratto and Inzolia, is a golden-colored, dry wine. The red, from Perricone and other varieties, is light and dry.

Fontana Murata, Bianco and Rosso, are made from the same grapes as the previous two wines and are quite similar in style. The Bianco in particular is quite good. At a recent tasting of Sicilian wines, it got high marks.

MARSALA

Now we turn our attention to the most renowned wine of Sicily, and indeed, one of the greatest of the fortified wines of the world—Marsala.

The name Marsala is taken from the town of that name in the area of its production. The town got its name from the Arabic *Marsh-El-Allah* (Harbor of God). Sicily was controlled for many years by the Saracens, and it was the Saracens, among its many ruling nations, who exerted the most profound influence on the island. It is fitting that they are responsible for the name of this, the outstanding viticultural product of Sicily.

Marsala is the product of Catarratto and/or Grillo grapes, with the addition of up to 15% Inzolia allowed. These grapes must be grown in or near those communes defined in the ministerial decree of October 1931 (updated November 1950). These communes, between Trapani and Marsala, are within the provinces of Agrigento, Palermo, and Trapani at the extreme western end of the island.

Marsala, as a fortified wine, was an accidental development of the seventeenth century. Shipments of wine from this area were sent to England. To prevent the wine from spoiling on its rough journey, in the sometimes steaming-hot hold of the ship, one part alcohol was added to fifty parts of the wine. This higher alcoholic content stabilized and helped to preserve the quality of the wine.

In the latter part of the eighteenth century, an English merchant, John Woodhouse, on a trip to Sicily, noticed Marsala's similarity to Madeira and sherry. The grapes grew in a similar climate—very hot and dry—in comparable soil, and had the high alcoholic content.

In 1773, he set up a concern and began to improve the archaic methods of viticulture and vinification. Following his lead, others, such as Inghams and Whittakers, also began making Marsala. Benjamin Ingham was the one who refined and modernized the technique for making Marsala.

Since that time, a *consorzio* has been organized to protect the wine and its reputation. The Consorzio per la Tutela del Vino Marsala awards a numbered neck label depicting an outline of Sicily in red to qualified wines.

Marsala results from the combination of (1) dry white wine, (2) concentrated must, and (3) heated must. (All of these components are subject to the regulations cited above regarding the allowable grapes and area of production.)

First a dry white wine is produced; next, a mixture consisting of one fourth wine brandy and three fourths *passito* wine (from semidried grapes) is added to the base in the proportion of six to one hundred—mixture to base. The heated must *(mistella)* is then added to this combination in the same proportions—six parts mixture to 100 parts base. The *mistella* is young unfermented grape juice which has been heated slowly until it takes on characteristics similar to caramel syrup: it becomes thick and sweet. This combination is left to age in red-oak casks for between four months and five years.

The resultant wine has a deep brown hue and a dry flavor with an underlying sweetness, and richness—a most interesting combination. With age, this sweetness diminishes. The aftertaste (finish) on Marsala can be very complex and lingering.

Marsala is classified into the following types:

Marsala Fine or I.P. (Italia Particolare)
Marsala Superiore, L.P., S.O.M. (Superiore Old Marsala), or G.D. (Garibaldi Dolce)

Marsala Vergine
Marsala Speciale

DOC requires Marsala Fine to be aged for at least four months and to be no less than 17% alcohol.

Marsala Superiore must be aged for two years and attain 18% alcohol.

Marsala Vergine must be no less than 18% alcohol and the original wine must have been aged a minimum of five years. This wine is made by the Solera System, whereby younger vintages are added to older ones. The bottle will contain a proportion of older vintages, but the youngest wine must have at least five years of barrel age.

Marsala Speciale must be at least 18% alcohol and cannot be sold prior to the July following the vintage. To the basic Marsala various flavors are added, such as almond cream, strawberry, cherry, banana, etc. But the most famous is Zabaglione. This is made by blending Marsala with egg yolks. A more commercial version of Zabaglione is Marsala Uovo or all' Uovo.

SICILIAN REDS

Available for less than $2 to around $3.

> **Regaleali Count Tasca
> Corvo Duca di Salaparuta
> Draceno Agricoltori Saturnia
> Drepano Agricoltori Saturnia
> Partinico
> Saturno Agricoltori Saturnia
> Segesta Rallo
> Villagrande Etna

SICILIAN WHITES

While most are about $2, a few run closer to $3.

*Corvo Duca di Salaparuta
*Regaleali Count Tasca
*Villagrande Etna
Draceno Agricoltori Saturnia
Drepano Agricoltori Saturnia
Partinico
Saturno Agricoltori Saturnia
Segesta Rallo

OTHER SICILIAN WINES

These wines are priced from about $2.50 to nearly $4.

*Malvasia di Lipari, Schiavo
Draceno Rose Agricoltori Saturnia
Regaleali Rose Count Tasca

MARSALA

From about $2.50 to about $3.50.

**Florio White Label Dry
*Florio White Label Sweet
*Rallo Black Label
*Rallo Superior Dry
Beccaro
Calamia Garibaldi Dolce
Calamia Italia Particulare Dry
Rallo Superior Sweet
Sicilian Gold Dry
Sicilian Gold Sweet

Stock Cream
Perlino Dry
Perlino Sweet

MARSALA SPECIALE

Most of these are in the $3 to $4 range.

**Florio Almond Cream
**Rallo Sun Drops Almond Cream
*Rallo Sun Drops Strawberry
*Rallo Sun Drops VSEP Sweet
Beccaro Almond Cream
Beccaro Cherry
Beccaro Coffee
Beccaro Mandarin
Beccaro Orange
Beccaro Sambuca
Beccaro Strawberry
Beccaro Walnut
Calamia Crema all'Uovo
Florio Floriovo (with egg)
Florio Golden Cream
Rallo Sun Drops Cremova Egg
Sicilian Gold Banana
Sicilian Gold Blackberry
Sicilian Gold Cream Coffee
Sicilian Gold Cremova
Sicilian Gold Mandarino
Sicilian Gold Mandocrema
Sicilian Gold Strawberry

SARDINIA

According to Waverly Root, legend tells us that after God had made the world, he had some bare rock and thin soil left over. Not wanting to waste it, he tossed it into the Mediterranean and pressed it down with his foot. And Sardinia does indeed have a footlike outline. In fact, it was originally named Ichnusa from the Greek *ikhnos* meaning "in the shape of a footprint."

Sardinia is one of the most intriguing places to visit. It is a land where, it seems, time stood still. The people continue to wear the old folk costumes. Many monuments still exist from the Stone Age and even earlier.

There are over 7000 nuraghi, prehistoric stone structures. These structures were made by piling blocks of stone in layers, one atop the other, without the use of mortar. Among the more fascinating ones—Nuraghe Losa, which stands three stories high and is fitted with built-in closets(!); Serra Orios, a village of seventy nuraghi laid out in blocks, with streets, some of them paved, and squares. On the squares are temples. And Nuraxi, a city of nuraghi believed to date from the thirteenth century B.C., dominated by a large stone fortress, can be seen at Burumini.

The tombs of giants, *domus de janas,* are believed to be even older than the nuraghi. These artificial caves were used as burial places. And there are structures which are even older. But enough—this is a book about wine, and what does all this have to do with wine!

Little of the wine of Sardinia is available in the United

States. But there is a good chance that some of the more interesting wines will be imported in the coming months, or at most in a few years.

Generally, the wines are heavy and alcoholic. The deep-colored reds are referred to as *vini neri* (black wines). The vines are trained *ab alberello*, close to the ground. The grapes, as a result, contain more sugar, the wines, more alcohol.

Cagliari, viticulturally as well as for many other reasons, is the most important province on the island. This province covers all of the southern portion and part of the east coast. Most of the DOC wines are from this province.

Most of the more interesting wines are sweet and go well with dessert.

CANNONAU DI SARDEGNA

Cannonau, a DOC wine made from grapes of the same name, is available in many types. Its flavor ranges from dry to sweet. Generally it is a strong, deep-ruby-colored wine that ends with a faint bitterness. Alcoholic minimum for this wine is 13.5%. Secco Superiore must attain 15% alcohol, Amabile Superiore, 14%, and Dolce Superiore, 13% alcohol.

There seems to be some argument concerning the drier version (which I have never tasted). Some writers describe it as common and suitable for blending; others claim that it is magnificent! Perhaps the truth lies somewhere in between.

Usually aged for a year in wood, with two additional years it may be labeled Riserva.

The sweeter versions go well with dessert.

GIRÒ DI CAGLIARI

Girò di Cagliari, another DOC wine, is the product of Girò grapes grown on the hills in the vicinity of Cagliari. This red wine has an intensely rich aroma and is full in body and flavor. It is highly alcoholic, usually ranging from 16 to 17%. A *liquoroso* version, at least 17.5% alcohol, that has been aged three years in wood may be labeled Riserva.

MONICA DI CAGLIARI

Monica di Cagliari, another sweet dessert wine, has also been awarded a DOC. This wine, made from Monica grapes (5% of other varieties also allowed), is similar to Girò, only deeper in color. It also has a wider alcoholic range—15 to 18%. If aged for three years in cask, it may be labeled Riserva.

MALVASIA DI CAGLIARI

Malvasia di Cagliari, also a DOC wine, is semisweet and 15 to 18% alcohol. The color is yellow to amber, and it is supposed to have an aftertaste of bitter almonds.

MOSCATO DI CAGLIARI

Moscato di Cagliari, from Moscatello Bianco grapes (5% of other varieties also allowed) grown on the hills around the plain of Campidano, is a golden-colored dessert wine of at least 16% alcohol. The *liquoroso*, with a year in wood and 17.5% alcohol, can be labeled Riserva. A *spumante* version also exists.

NASCO DI CAGLIARI

Nasco di Cagliari, from Nasco grapes (up to 5% of other varieties allowed) is another DOC dessert wine. It is golden in color with a delicate aroma and a slight bitterness at the end. The grapevines are planted around the Campidano plain.

VERNACCIA DI ORISTANO

Now we turn to the most interesting of all Sardinian wines—Vernaccia di Oristano. This wine, too, has been granted a DOC, and is named for the grapes from which it is made. The grapes are planted near Oristano in the lower Tirso Valley.

This amber-colored wine has an intense aroma that recalls almonds. It is rich and very dry on the palate, and similar to sherry, except that it is unfortified. It must be aged two years in wood, but with an additional year and 15.5% alcohol it may be labeled Superiore. This wine improves with age.

It is a suitable accompaniment to seafood, shellfish.

COUNTRY AND JUG WINES

The following wines, although tending to be inexpensive, are not necessarily inferior. Some of them are better than other wines not offered in jug. Their larger container and smaller price make them especially suitable for picnics and parties.

If you buy a jug and don't finish it, you can pour the remaining wine into smaller bottles, cork tightly, and put away until you are ready to drink it. If the amount left doesn't fill your smallest bottles, drop in marbles (and you thought they were only for kids!) in order to top up the wine.

Some of these wines are offered in smaller sizes as well, and others come in even larger sizes.

As in the previous sections, an asterisk(*) indicates a good buy. It means a good wine, true to its type. As I haven't tasted all of these wines, the absence of the star should not be taken as a mark against the wine.

CHIANTI

Most of these wines are in the $3.50 to $4.50 range, with some retailing for more—a handful command more than $6.

	ounces		ounces
Bardi	64	Bruni	64
Barsottini	64	Bruni Black Label	50
Borghini	64	Buitoni	64
Brolio Misura		Cavalier	64
Chiantigiana	59	Certaldo Castel	64

	ounces		ounces
Certaldo Opici	59	Pietrini	64
Certaldo Valbella	64	Pillo	64
Conte Vecchio	64	Raspollini	64
Fassati Valdoro	60	Ricasoli	64
Felini	128	Ruffino	64
Frescobaldi	64	Ruffino Misura	
Giannozzi	50	Chiantigiana	59
Graziosi	64	Sardelli	64
Magni	64	Serristori	64
Marca Verde	64	Spada	128
Melini	64	Torre	128
Mirafiore	64	Victori	64

CHIANTI CLASSICO

These wines range from about $4 to about $6.50.

	ounces
*Soderi	50
Antinori Santa Christina	59
Brolio	64
Cappelli	64
Cecchi	50
Suali	64
Verrazzano	50

VERONESE WINES

BARDOLINO, VALPOLICELLA, AND SOAVE

Most of these range from about $2.50 to about $4.50; a few go for approximately $7.50.

	ounces		*ounces*
*Bertani	64	Petternella	48
*Lamberti	59	Riva del Garda	50
*Ruffino	64	Sangiorgio	68
Bolla	64	Sterzi	51
Bosca	50	Tytell	51
Buitoni	64	Vallene	50
Canova	50	Villa Maria	50
Livio	50	Villa Pinza	64
Murari	50	Zonin	58

LAMBRUSCO

Most of these are in the $3 to $4 range, but a couple go for about $4.50.

	ounces
Baroncini	50
Bosca	50
Cella	50
Giacobazzi	50
Gioia	52
Livio	51
Mandia	59
Riunite	48
Sant'Anna	59
Sardelli Dragone	58
Zonin	50

LAMBRUSCO-TYPE ROSES

Most of these wines are in the $3 to $4 price range, but some are priced at about $4.50.

ounces

Baroncini	50
Giacobazzi	50
Gioia	52
Riunite	48

LAMBRUSCO-TYPE WHITES

Most are in the $3 to $4 price range, but some go for about $4.50.

ounces

Baroncini	50
Giacobazzi	50
Riunite	48
Zonin	50

OTHER REDS

While most of these jugs are in the $2.50 to $3.50 range, some go as high as about $5.

ounces

**Casal Thaulero Montepulciano	60
*Pavan Italian Country	64
Barberini Castelli Romani	67
Barbero Barberg Barbera d'Alba	68
Barbero Barberg Freisa del Piemonte	68
Barbero Barberg Grignolino	68
Bersano Barbera	50

	ounces
Borghini Camel Palline	64
Bosca Barbera	50
Cantine Sociale Colli Albani	
Castelli Romani	68
Castellano Barbera	128
Comandini Castelli Romani	68
Cossetti Barbera	59
de Sanctis Castelli Romani	50
FPV Vino Rosso (Verona)	50
Grifoni Tuscan Red	64
Kettmeir Lago di Caldaro	50
Livio Cabernet Sauvignon	51
Marino Rubino	60
Marchese Villadoria Barbera	50
Marchese Villadoria Dolcetto	50
Marchese Villadoria Grignolino	50
Marchese Villadoria Nebbiolo	50
Partinico Sicilian Red	68
Podere Miloc (Angoris) Cabernet	50
Podere Miloc (Angoris) Merlot	50
Rallo Segesta	68
Rusticano	68
Sangiorgio Merlot	68
Valtinera Barbera	68
Valtinera Freisa	59
Villa Banfi	64
Villa Maria	50
Zamboni Barbera d'Asti	59
Zamboni Brachetto	68

OTHER ROSES

Most of these jugs are in the $2.50 to $3.50 price range, but some go as high as about $5.

	ounces
Antinori Rose di Bolgheri	59
Barberini Castelli Romani	67
Bigi	64
Bolla	59
FPV Vino Rose (Verona)	50
Marino Roman Country Rose	60
Pavan	64
Villa Banfi	64

OTHER WHITES

Most of these are available at from $2.50 to about $4; a few cost over $6.

	ounces
**Villa Maria	50
*Marino	60
Antinori Orvieto	59
Barberini Castelli Romani	67
Cantine Sociale Colli Albani	68
Cappelli Bianco	64
Casal Thaulero Trebbiano	60
Comandini Frascati	68
de Sanctis Castelli Romani	50
Fassati Bianco Valdoro	60

	ounces
FPV Vino Bianco (Verona)	50
Kettmeir Pinot Bianco	50
Marca Verde	64
Marino Frascati	68
Mirafiore	64
Partinico Sicilian White	68
Pavan Country White	64
Podere Miloc (Angoris) Pinot Bianco	50
Podere Miloc (Angoris) Tocai	50
Rallo Segesta	68
Ruffino Tuscan White	64
Rusticano	68
San Giorgio Tocai	68
Villa Banfi	64
Zamboni Moscato	59
Zonin Trebbiano	50

SPECIALTY WINES

Most of these are in the $2 to $3 range, but some cost upwards of $4.50.

*Moscalba
*Spumarosa
 Albarosa
 Biancalba
 Frizzalba
 Frizzoro
 Rossalba
 Zanti Vino Bianco
 Zanti Vino Rosso

OF ARTICHOKES
AND OTHER THINGS

Some Italian alcoholic beverages are quite unusual; in their taste and in their ingredients, some are unique. These products deserve separate attention.

CYNAR

Foremost among these unusual beverages is Cynar, an artichoke-based apéritif. As long ago as 700 B.C. the artichoke was popular, due to the belief that it was a diuretic, and also an aphrodisiac. But it wasn't until 1951 that someone made a drink from it. In that year, Cynar was invented.

This versatile, bittersweet drink can be drunk before, during or after a meal. Before the meal it is an excellent apéritif, for two reasons. First, as with many other apéritifs, its bitterness helps to stimulate your digestive system and to whet your appetite; its second virtue is its taste-softening properties. According to Dr. Linda Bartoshuk, taste physiologist at Yale University, in *Science* magazine:

> To the best of our knowledge, the earliest published report of a taste-modifying property of the artichoke was Blakeslee's account of the 1934 A.A.A.S. biologists' dinner. After eating globe artichokes as the salad course, sixty percent of the nearly 250 people present reported that water tasted different—in most cases, it tasted sweet. Others have also noticed anec-

dotally that beverages, such as milk and wine, as well as water, taste sweet after the subjects have eaten artichokes.

Cynar can also be served during the meal with hot or spicy food. Hard as it may be to believe, mixed with Fresca, it goes surprisingly well with some Chinese dishes. Recently at a gourmet Chinese banquet this beverage, Cynar-Fresca, was served with Chinese vegetables. Many people remarked about the combination; the consensus was that it went very well.

And, because of its digestive quality, Cynar is a good after-dinner drink—either by itself or in combination with other ingredients, as Cynar-Crema (see below) or Cynet (Cynar with a dash of Fernet Branca).

Besides all of this versatility, this artichoke-based apéritif has other possibilities. At a recent Symposium on the Artichoke (at Polignano a Mare, Italy, in November 1973) it was shown that cynarin, one of the two active components of this vegetable, helps stimulate the regeneration of liver cells. It was pointed out that these cells are consumed more rapidly under stress. Hence the following expression with regard to Cynar—*Contro il logorio della vita moderna* (against the stress of modern living).

In another research paper, it was pointed out that cynarin helps to reduce the cholesterol level in the blood. While it has been proven that cynarin produces these desirable effects (regeneration of liver cells and the reduction of cholesterol), it has not yet been shown that Cynar has the same results. It is, nevertheless, a versatile and intriguing drink.

Cynar-Apéritif—2 oz. Cynar on the rocks and orange slice.
Cynar-Soda—2 oz. Cynar, 2 oz. soda, and orange slice.
Italiano—2 oz. Cynar, 2 oz. sweet Vermouth, ice, and orange slice.

Romano—1 oz. Cynar, 1 oz. gin, 1 oz. sweet Vermouth, ice, and orange slice.

Cynar-Fresca—2 oz. Cynar on ice, and Fresca to fill glass.

Buona Notte—2 oz. Cynar and cold fresh milk to fill glass.

Cynar-Crema—1½ oz. heated Cynar, over which ½ oz. heavy cream is poured slowly on a teaspoon held bottom side up to float over the Cynar.

TUACA

Tuaca is a most unusual beverage: it has an aroma and flavor of butterscotch. The similarity is created from a blend of brandy, milk, and vanilla. Delicious by itself, it is also a delightful addition to coffee.

GIN

This next drink, while not unusual in itself, is unusual to be made in Italy (unexpected, at any rate). Romantico and Gladiator Gin are available in this country. Gin is a grain spirit which gets its distinctive flavor from juniper berries. The alcohol is from distilled grain; the flavor, from the berries. When we think of gin, we tend to think of England and Holland, but now you can get gin from Italy as well. Seems a natural with Italian Vermouth.

FIOR D'ALPI

Fior d'Alpi, "Flower of the Alps," is reportedly produced from the extract of flowers. Mille Fiori, they claim, is from the extract of a thousand flowers. The Isolabella is available in this country. This unusual liqueur is produced in the Italian Alps, as you may have guessed. Inside the tall, clear, flute-shaped bottle floats a twig encrusted with sugar crystals, which gives the impression of a Christmas tree. This liqueur is similar to Chartreuse, which is also said to use an extensive collection of plants in its composition.

STREGA LIQUORE

Strega Liquore is made with more than seventy herbs and barks. Legend has it that beautiful young maidens, in the guise of witches, originally mixed this magic brew in Benevento. According to tradition, if two people drink it together, they will be united forever. This yellow-colored liqueur is recommended with ice cream.

NOCINO

Another unusual drink is Nocino, a walnut-flavored liqueur. This liqueur is made from green walnuts in the province of Modena, in Emilia-Romagna.

The walnuts grow in the foothills of the Apennines between Sassuola and Formigine. Nocino was first produced in monasteries, but today it is made by large distilleries in Modena and Sassuola. Each has its own carefully guarded recipe. Basically, green walnuts with their empty shells are steeped in alcohol for two years. This mixture is then transferred to brown oak casks for a year of aging. The liquid is then distilled and bottled. The result is a delightfully walnut-flavored liqueur with a trace of bitterness.

AMARETTO

The origin of Amaretto is discovered in a charming, if apocryphal, tale: Bernardino Luini, the Renaissance painter, and a beautiful young widow head the cast in this story.

Luini had received the commission to paint the murals in the Sanctuary of Santa Maria della Grazia in the town of Saronno. During his stay in the town, while the work was in progress, he had taken rooms at the inn on Via Varesina, across from the sanctuary. One of the murals was to depict the Madonna and child, and Luini needed just the right model to sit for him. He was inspired to choose the young and attractive blond innkeeper, who was a recent widow and nursing a baby boy.

To express her gratitude at being so immortalized, the young woman wanted to give the artist a gift at Christmas. Not having the means to buy him a gift worthy of the honor, legend tells us, she created a special *liquore* for him, from almonds of apricots steeped in brandy. The result was a sweet, pleasing almond liqueur known since as Amaretto.

The most popular one today is the Amaretto di Saronno, a direct descendant, we are told, of that original *liquore* made by the grateful innkeeper of Saronno.

AQUA VITAE: WATER OF LIFE

Brandy is a spirit, and a spirit is the distillate of fruit, grain, or their by-products. Distillation is based on the principle that alcohol vaporizes at a lower temperature than water, due to the fact that it is lighter. These vapors are trapped and then condensed back into a liquid form. The resultant liquid has a higher alcoholic content than the original source.

Brandy, like wine, is a product of the grape. "Brandy" is short for "brandywine," meaning burnt (i.e., distilled) wine. Its precise meaning: the result of the distillation of wine or its by-product. The name brandy is often used to refer to the distillates of other fruits as well. But in this case the term will be qualified by the type of fruit, e.g., pear brandy, apple brandy, etc.

Brandy can be either distilled wine or distilled pomace. Pomace is the by-product of the crush. After the grapes are pressed, the juice is run off into a vat to ferment. The solid matter left behind (skins, stalks, etc.) can be distilled to make *marc* or *grappa*. This brandy is generally quite rough and coarse. But those who like it claim there is nothing finer. The name *grappa* is a shortened version of *grappolo di uva* (bunch of grapes).

A number of factors affecting the quality of brandy are:

(1) The grapes (the wine or pomace);
(2) Distillation;
(3) The period and conditions of aging;
(4) The wood in which the brandy is aged.

170

Brandy is thought to have originated in the thirteenth century; it is known that wine was distilled during that time. Arnaldo da Villanova, born in Spain in 1238 and educated in Sicily, gave brandy its name, *acqua di vite* (vine water). This was later changed to *aqua vitae* (water of life).

BRANDY (GRAPPA)

Italian brandies range from about $6 to about $7.50.

*Cavaglio Grappa, 84 proof
Kiola Grappa del Piemonte, 84 proof
Monquin Italian Brandy, 10 years old, 80 proof
Royal Stock, 10 years old, 86.8 proof
Stock Grappa, 90 proof
Stock "84" Gran Riserva, 10 years old, 80 proof
Vecchia Romagna Brandy, 80 proof

LIQUORE

A liqueur is a sweet-flavored alcoholic beverage. These cordials, as we call them in the United States, are normally drunk at the end of a meal. Italy, where they are called *aqua ardens* (which may be very loosely translated "fire water"), like many other countries, produces a wide variety of them.

Generally, liqueurs are a combination of spirits, sugar, and syrup flavored with fruits, herbs, and/or other plants.

Distillation of aromatic liquids and of water was known to the ancients; but as a process applied to alcoholic beverages, distillation is believed to have been invented about 900 A.D. by the Arabs.

The art of liqueur-making was practiced by the alchemists. But the art of modern liqueur-making, which combines the aromas of fruits and vegetables with brandy *(aqua ardens composita)*, is believed to have been originated in the early part of the fifteenth century by G. M. Savonarola. Savonarola, a doctor at Padua, had a young patient, the beautiful mistress of one of the town's leading noblemen. She complained of feeling ill. The doctor combined honey and attar of roses with brandy as his prescription for her. Soon all of her friends were claiming illness in order to get some of this wonderful medicine, "Rosolio," which was the first known liqueur.

In 1532, when Catherine de' Medici went to France to marry the Duke of Orleans, who later became Henri II, she took with her, besides her chefs, some of Italy's leading liqueur-makers. Thus, liqueur-making was imported along with the art of cooking into France.

172

Two general processes are used to make liqueurs—distillation and maceration. Distillation has been discussed in brief under brandy. Maceration, or infusion, is a process in which herbs, plants, or similar ingredients are left to steep in an alcoholic base. The result is that some of the flavor from these ingredients is imparted to the alcohol, and a liqueur is born. This process is normally used for more delicate ingredients, i.e., those that would be hurt by the heat of distillation.

Over $8
**Cora Blasius Liquore d'Erbe
 *Amaretto di Saronno, 56 proof (23 oz.)
 *Aurum Orange Liqueur, 78 proof (25 oz.)
 *Sambuca Molinari, 84 proof (25.6 oz.)
 *Tuaca Demi Sec Milk Brandy (23 oz.)
  Liqueur Strega, 80 proof (23 oz.)
  Liquore Galliano, 80 proof (23 oz.)
  Martini & Rossi Lixy Chianamartini, 62 proof (23 oz.)
  Patrician Sambuca, 80 proof (fifth)
  Sambuca Originale, 84 proof (fifth)
  Sambuca Romana, 84 proof (23 oz.)

Between $6.50 and $8
 *Patrician Amaretto, 48 proof (fifth)
  Campari Liqueur, 72 proof (25 oz.)
  Ciao Ciao, 80 proof (23 oz.)
  Expresso Coffee Liqueur, 60 proof (fifth)
  Isobella Fior d'Alpi, 92 proof (23 oz.)
  Mocchia Amaretto di Ferraro, 56 proof (23.6 oz.)
  Mocchia Sambuca Italia, 80 proof (23.6 oz.)
  Patrician Amaro, 48 proof (fifth)
  Patrician Anisette, 48 proof (fifth)
  Patrician Cedrino, 48 proof (fifth)
  Patrician Cherry, 48 proof (fifth)

Patrician Mocarino, 48 proof (fifth)
Patrician Nocino, 48 proof (fifth)
Sambuca di Trevi, 84 proof (24 oz.)
Stock Cherristock, 50 proof (fifth)
Stock Liquore Roiana, 80 proof (fifth)

Between $5 and $6.50
Cora Amaro
Drioli Apricot, 62 proof (fifth)
Drioli Cherry, 62 proof (fifth)
Drioli Coffee, 62 proof (fifth)
Drioli Maraschino, 64 proof (fifth)
Drioli Triple Sec, 62 proof (fifth)
Stock Anesone, 90 proof (fifth)
Stock Bora (Sambuca type), 70 proof (fifth)
Stock Galacafe, 70 proof (fifth)

Between $3.50 and $5
*Patrician Samoca, 80 proof (fifth)
Patrician Cedrino, 80 proof (fifth)
Patrician Nocino, 80 proof (fifth)
Stock Anisette, 60 proof (fifth)
Stock Apricot, 60 proof (fifth)
Stock Blackberry, 60 proof (fifth)
Stock Coffee Espresso (Moca), 60 proof (fifth)
Stock Creme de Cacao, light and dark, 60 proof (fifth)
Stock Creme de Menthe, green and white, 60 proof (fifth)
Stock Curaçao, 60 proof (fifth)
Stock Kümmel, 60 proof (fifth)
Stock Mandarine, 60 proof (fifth)
Stock Maraschino, 60 proof (fifth)
Stock Peach, 60 proof (fifth)
Stock Peppermint Schnapps, 60 proof (fifth)

Stock Prunella, 60 proof (fifth)
Stock Rosolio, 60 proof (fifth)
Stock Triple Sec, 60 proof (fifth)

Under $3.50
Apricot Julep, 36 proof (fifth)
Blackberry Julep, 40 proof (fifth)
Cherry Julep, 40 proof (fifth)
Volare Aperitivo, 34 proof (fifth)

APERITIVI

**Cynar
*Jolly
Cora Americano
Punt e Mes

AROMATIC BITTERS

*Fernet Branca
Campari

SERVING: SUGGESTED ACCOMPANIMENTS

The following tables offer serving tips—certain types of food with complementary wines. These are only suggestions; they offer a guideline. They're not meant to be followed ritualistically. Do not drink red wine with steaks because you are told that that is correct. It is *not* correct. What is correct is what tastes good to you. We are not dealing with morality. Be subjective—drink and eat what suits your taste.

These combinations, certain wines with certain kinds of food, have resulted because of the affinity between particular flavors in the wines and the foods. As an example, a robust red wine has a strong enough flavor to complement the gamy flavor of venison, while a light red would be overpowered by it. However, if you prefer a light red wine, drink it.

Again, a strong red wine would overpower the delicate flavor of lobster, while the delicacy, dryness, and effervescence of a Brut Spumante seems to combine with it in a perfect marriage of flavors. But if you like lobster with red wine, by all means drink red wine. ("Red wine with red fish, and white wine with . . .") It's your palate. *Ognuno a suo gusto.*

BEFORE THE MEAL

Aperitivo (Apéritif)
Brut Spumante
Crisp, dry white wine
Dry, fortified wine

APERITIVO
Cynar
Punt e Mes
Vermouth, dry or Bianco

BRUT SPUMANTE
Antinori Brut
Calissano Duca d'Alba
Carpene Malvolti Brut
Cinzano Brut
Cora Brut
Franco Brut

CRISP, DRY WHITE WINE
Blanc de Morgex
Castel Byria
Castel Chiuro
Orvieto Secco
Pinot Grigio
Prosecco (still, dry)
Soave
Sylvaner
Verdicchio

DRY, FORTIFIED WINE
Marsala

HORS D'OEUVRE—ANTIPASTO

FISH-BASED
Brut Spumante
Dry white wine, crisp or fruity

MEAT-BASED
Light red wine

MIXTURE
Brut Spumante
Rosato (rosé)

BRUT SPUMANTE
Antinori Brut
Calissano Duca d'Alba
Carpene Malvolti Brut
Cinzano Brut
Cora Brut
Franco Brut

DRY WHITE WINE, CRISP OR FRUITY
Albana di Romagna
Blanc de Morgex
Castel Byria
Castel Chiuro
Castel del Monte Bianco
Castelli Romani Bianco
Cortese
Frascati
Lugana
Malvasia
Orvieto Secco

Pinot Bianco
Pinot Grigio
Prosecco (still, dry)
Ravello Bianco
Rhine Riesling
Ribolla
Riesling Italico
Sauvignon
Soave
Sylvaner
Terlano
Tocai (di Lison)
Torgiano
Traminer
Trebbiano d'Abruzzo
Trebbiano di Romagna
The Tuscan whites
Velletri
Verdicchio

LIGHT RED WINE
Bardolino
Castelli Romani Rosso
Chianti (*governo* type)
Dolcetto
Freisa
Grauernatsch
Grignolino
Merlot
Rosso Conero
Rosso Piceno
Valgella
Valpolicella

ROSATO
Brachetto Rose
Castel del Monte Rosato
Castelli Romani Rosato
Chiaretto del Garde Rosato
Lison Rose
The Marche roses
Ravello Rosato
Rosatello
Rosato di Bolgheri
Rosato di Verona
Rosato Raboso
Rose del Golfo
Rose Reale
Selvanella Rose
The Tuscan roses
The Umbrian roses

SEAFOOD AND FISH

FRESH-WATER FISH—FRIED, GRILLED
Light, fruity white wine

SALT-WATER FISH—FRIED, GRILLED (DELICATE FLAVOR)
Fruity white wine

SALT-WATER FISH—FRIED, GRILLED (STRONG FLAVOR)
Dry, crisp white wine

SHELLFISH
Crisp, dry white wine
Brut Spumante

FISH OR SHELLFISH WITH SAUCE
Depends on the sauce

FRESH-WATER OR (DELICATELY FLAVORED) SALT-WATER FISH
Blanc de Morgex
Colli Albani
Colli Lanuvini
Cortese
Est! Est!! Est!!!
Frascati
Lugana
Orvieto
Pinot Bianco
Ribolla
Sylvaner

SHELLFISH OR SALT-WATER FISH
Albana di Romagna
Biancolella
Castel Byria
Castel Chiuro
Cinqueterre
Frecciarossa
Ischia Bianco
Lacrima Christi
Malvasia
Orvieto
Pinot Bianco
Pinot Grigio
Riesling Italico
Sauvignon
Scandiano Bianco
Soave

Terlano
Trebbiano d'Abruzzo
Trebbiano di Romagna
The Tuscan whites
Verdicchio
Vernaccia di Oristano

BRUT SPUMANTE
Antinori Brut
Calissano Duca d'Alba
Carpene Malvolti Brut
Cinzano Brut
Cora Brut
Franco Brut

SAUSAGES AND COLD MEATS

SAUSAGES
Dolcetto
Grauernatsch
Grignolino

COLD WHITE MEATS, COLD CUTS
Torgiano Bianco
Verdicchio

COLD RED MEATS
Cabernet

PASTA AND RISOTTO

Generally, the sauce determines the wine.

LIGHT OR CREAMY SAUCE
Light red wine

RICH SAUCE
Full red wine

SPICY SAUCE
Robust red wine

SEAFOOD SAUCE (WITH HEAVY SPICE)
Spicy white wine

SEAFOOD SAUCE (WITHOUT HEAVY SPICE)
Full-bodied white wine

LIGHT OR CREAMY SAUCE
Bardolino
Castelli Romani Rosso
Chianti (*governo* type)
Dolcetto
Freisa
Grauernatsch
Grignolino
Merlot
Rosso Conero
Rosso Piceno
Valgella
Valpolicella

Rich Sauce
Castel Chiuro Riserva
Carema
Donnaz
Fracia
Gattinara
Ghemme
Grumello
Inferno
Sassella
Spanna
Torre Quarto

Spicy Sauce
Aglianico del Vulture
Amarone
Barbaresco
Barbera
Barolo
Cirò
Sfursat

Seafood Sauce (With Heavy Spice)
Gewürztraminer
Traminer

Seafood Sauce (Without Heavy Spice)
Albana di Romagna
Castel Chiuro
Colli Albani
Colli Lanuvini
Frascati

Pinot Bianco
Riesling Italico
Sauvignon

POULTRY AND WILD FOWL

CHICKEN
Fruity white, light red

TURKEY
Full white, medium red

DUCK
Full red

WILD FOWL
Robust red

WELL-SEASONED FOWL
Robust red

CHICKEN
Bardolino
Chianti (*governo* type)
Dolcetto
Freisa
Grignolino
Kalterersee
Lago di Caldaro
Malvasia
Orvieto
Trebbiano d'Abruzzo

Trebbiano di Romagna
Valgella
Valpolicella

TURKEY
Carema
Donnaz
Etna Rosso
Ghemme
Merlot
Montepulciano d'Abruzzo
Ravello
Torgiano
Spanna

DUCK
Barbaresco
Barbera
Pinot Noir
Valtellina Superiore

WILD FOWL
Barbaresco
Castel Chiuro Riserva
Gattinara
Spanna
Torre Quarto
Valtellina Superiore

WELL-SEASONED FOWL
Amarone
Barolo
Cirò
Sfursat

WHITE MEAT: VEAL AND PORK

Medium white wine
Light or medium red wine
Highly seasoned dishes call for a full red wine.

Bardolino
Cabernet Sauvignon
Carema
Dolceacqua
Donnaz
Frecciarossa
Freisa
Ghemme
Kalterersee
Lacrima Christi Rosso
Lago di Caldaro
Lagrein Dunkel
Merlot
Montepulciano d'Abruzzo
Pinot Noir
Ravello Rosso
Refosco
Rosso Conero
Rosso Piceno
Valgella
Valpolicella

RED MEAT: BEEF AND LAMB

STEAKS AND CHOPS
Medium to full red wine

Stews, Braised and Boiled Meats
Full common red wine

Roasts (Oven and Pot)
Full or robust red wine

Steaks and Chops
Cabernet
Castel del Monte Rosso
Chianti Classico Riserva
Fracia
Gattinara
Ghemme
Groppello
Merlot
Pinot Noir
Sangiovese di Romagna
Santa Maddalena
Spanna
Torgiano Rosso
Torre Quarto

Stews, Braised and Boiled Meats
Barbera
Ischia Rosso

Roasts (Oven and Pot)
Amarone
Barbaresco
Barolo
Brunello di Montalcino
Castel Chiuro Riserva
Castel del Monte, Fasciarossa
Cirò

Gattinara
Grumello
Inferno
Per' 'e Palummo
Pinot Noir
Sassella
Vino Nobile di Montepulciano

GAME

Full robust red wine

Aglianico del Vulture
Amarone
Barbaresco
Barolo
Brunello di Montalcino
Castel Chiuro Riserva
Cirò
Gattinara
Grumello
Inferno
Per' 'e Palummo
Sassella
Vino Nobile di Montepulciano

FRUIT AND DESSERT

Albana di Romagna
Asti Spumante
Brachetto Spumante
Cannonau di Sardegna

Cinqueterre
Giro di Cagliari
Malvasia di Cagliari
Malvasia di Lipari
Marsala Speciale
Marsala, sweet
Monica di Cagliari
Moscato di Cagliari
Moscato di Pantelleria
Moscato di Siracusa
Moscato Naturale d'Asti
Nasco di Cagliari
Prosecco Spumante
Recioto Bianco
Recioto di Soave
Verduzzo
Vin Santo

It has been my experience that no wine really goes with ice cream; for this, try a liqueur.

SERVING: BREATHING THE WINE

The following breathing times are intended as a guideline; they cannot be given to the minute, as wines vary. These times apply to young wines. Older wines generally need less air, as they contain less tannin; and venerable old vintages could fade from too much air.

Since decanting exposes the wine to more air, when this is done the suggested times should be shortened.

It is a wise idea when breathing a wine you're unfamiliar with to test the wine from time to time to see how it's developing. If it seems to come around too soon—before you're ready to drink it—you can simply put the cork (stopper) back in to hold it.

LESS THAN ONE HOUR

Many of these wines are light-bodied and common, others are a bit sharp. In these cases, the wines can be served slightly chilled.

Bardolino	Montepulciano d'Abruzzo
The Castelli Romani reds	Nebbiolo
Chianti (*governo* type)	Ravello Rosso
Dolcetto	Rosso Conero
Freisa	Rosso Piceno
Grauernatsch	Segesta Red
Grignolino	The Tuscan reds
Lacrima Christi Rosso	Valgella
Lago di Caldaro	Valpolicella
Kalterersee	All country and jug wines
The Marche reds	

ONE HOUR

The Alto Adige reds:
  Cabernet Sauvignon
  Lagrein Dunkel
  Merlot
  Pinot Noir
  Santa Maddalena
Chianti
Classico Chianti
Corvo
Fracia
The Friuli Venezia
  Giulia reds:
  Cabernet

Merlot
Mont Quarin Rose
Pinot Nero
Refosco
Groppello
The Piave River reds:
  Cabernet
  Merlot
  Pinot Nero
  Rubino
  Sangiovese
  Torre Quarto

TWO HOURS

Barbaresco
Barbera
Carema
Castel Chiuro Riserva
Castel del Monte
Classico Chianti Riserva
Frecciarossa

Ghemme
Grumello
Inferno
Per' 'e Palummo
Sassella
Spanna
Torgiano (Rubesco)

FOUR HOURS

†Aglianico del Vulture
†Amarone
†Barolo
†Brunello di Montalcino
  Cirò
  Gattinara

†Groppello Amarone
Rivera Fasciarossa
  (Castel del Monte)
Valpolicella Amarone
Vino Nobile di
  Montepulciano

†Even longer wouldn't hurt.

FRENCH AND ITALIAN WINE EQUIVALENTS

In this era of rising wine prices it is helpful to be able to substitute a lower-priced wine for a higher-priced one. But to do this we must have some knowledge of what is substitutable. The following table, like the others in this book, offers a guideline. Considering the characteristics of a particular French wine, one or more somewhat reasonable Italian substitutes have been suggested.

It must be emphasized, however, that *no two wines are the same*, especially if they are from different areas. Just as the Riservas of Classico Chianti differ from the chateaux of the Haut Médoc, so do the chateaux of Pauillac differ from those of Margaux. Nevertheless, these wines do have a similarity, in delicacy and structure. Many experts have mistaken the great Chianti Classico Riservas for major chateaux of the Haut Médoc.

This is *not* to say that these wines should be compared— *they should not*. The great Italian wines and the great French wines have their own personalities, and should each be taken on its own merits. But there is sufficient similarity structurally to allow one to say, "Oh, you like the great Rhône wines of Hermitage and Côte Rôtie; well, the great Piedmontese wines, Barolo and Barbaresco, have a similar robustness and forthrightness of character that you should enjoy."

But in the final analysis, you must decide, and I am attempting to help by providing a guideline. *In vino veritas.*

FRENCH	ITALIAN
Alsace:	Alto Adige:
Traminer	Gewürztraminer
Riesling	Rhein Riesling
Sylvaner	Sylvaner
	Friuli-Venezia Giulia:
Sylvaner	Riesling Italico
Tocai	Tocai
Traminer	Traminer
Bordeaux:	
Major chateaux of northern	Mature Gattinara
Haut Médoc:	"Vallana" Spanna
Pauillac, St. Estèphe, etc.	Frecciarossa Grand Cru
	Brunello di Montalcino
	Vino Nobile
	di Montepulciano
	Inferno
	Valgella
Major chateaux of southern	Classico Chianti Riserva
Haut Médoc:	Torgiano (Rubesco)
St. Julien, Margaux, etc.	
Minor chateaux of	Chianti
Haut Médoc	Classico Chianti
	Cabernet Sauvignon (Alto Adige)
	Lagrein Dunkel
	Santa Maddalena

FRENCH	ITALIAN
St. Emilion, Pomerol	Castel del Monte (Rosso) Torre Quarto Young Gattinara Ghemme Spanna Grumello Sassella
Bourg, Blaye, Bordeaux Supérieur	Sangiovese di Romagna Cabernet (Friuli- Venezia Giulia) Merlot (Alto Adige) Chianti
Graves (white), Entre Deux Mers	Trebbiano di Romagna Lacrima Christi
Burgundy: Côtes d'Or (red)	Carema Castel Chiuro Riserva Fracia
Côtes d'Or (white)	Castel Byria Pinot Castel Chiuro Soave
Chalonnais (red)	Pinot Nero (Friuli-Venezia Giulia) Pinot Noir (Alto Adige) Valpolicella

FRENCH	ITALIAN
Mâconnais (white)	Pinot Grigio Some Tuscan whites (notably that of Ruffino)
Beaujolais: Beaujolais Supérieur, Brouilly, etc.	Dolcetto Freisa Grignolino Bardolino
Morgon, Moulin-à-Vent	Dolcetto Freisa
Côtes du Rhône: Northern Côtes du Rhone, including Hermitage and Côte Rôtie	Barolo Barbaresco Cirò Aglianico del Vulture Sfursat Groppello Amarone Recioto Amarone
Southern Côtes du Rhône, including Châteauneuf-du-Pape, common Côtes du Rhône, and Côtes du Rhône Villages	Barbera Nebbiolo Groppello Some Sicilian reds
Loire (red)	Lago di Caldaro Kalterersee Rosso Conero Rosso Piceno

FRENCH	ITALIAN
Loire (white)	Albana di Romagna
	Scandiano Bianco
	Orvieto
	Frascati
	Velletri
	The Tuscan whites
	Verdicchio
	Est! Est!! Est!!! di Monte- fiascone
	Ravello Bianco
	Blanc de Morgex
	Cortese
	Lugana
	Cinqueterre
	Pinot Bianco
	Terlano
	Prosecco (still)
	Tocai di Lison
	Malvasia
	Sauvignon
Loire (*mousseux*)	Prosecco Spumante
Champagne, Brut	Brut Spumante, Piedmont
	Brut Spumante, Venezia Euganea
	Brut Spumante, Tuscany
Côtes du Provence Rosé	Chiaretto del Garda
	The Tuscan roses

FRENCH	ITALIAN
Country wines (reds, whites, rosés)	Segesta
	Some Sicilian wines
	Pavan country wines
	Trebbiano d'Abruzzo
	Montepulciano d'Abruzzo
	Castelli Romani wines
	Colli Albani
	Colli Lanuvini
	Marino
	Ravello Rosso, Rosato

HOW TO LEARN MORE
ABOUT ITALIAN WINE

"The only way to learn about wines is to taste them, and there is no substitute for pulling a cork."

—ANDRÉ SIMON

What it comes down to is experience. This can be gained in three ways:

(1) Drinking wine in your own home or at a friend's, which first requires that you (or your friend) shop for the wine;

(2) Drinking wine with your meal in a restaurant, which first requires that you order the wine;

(3) Drinking wine at wine tastings, which only requires that you attend (and is made easier by joining a wine club).

You can also learn about wine by reading, but what you learn is more historical or theoretical. The most important thing about wine is how it tastes, so if you are thirsty for knowledge of wine, to really learn you must taste it.

In purchasing wine, you must first choose a store to shop in. Look around. Compare prices. Watch ads in newspapers and magazines. Read your newspaper wine column, if it is a consumer-oriented column. Request catalogues from local merchants. Finally, make your selection of one or more stores to shop in. Look for a merchant who knows his products, who is helpful, and, if you are looking for special wines, who will order them for you if he doesn't carry them.

199

In ordering wine in a restaurant, you require some knowledge of wine. This book should help. You can, in addition, take advantage of the wine knowledge of the staff in the restaurant, by getting suggestions from the waiter or *sommelier.*

There are two other major ways in which you can use a restaurant to increase your knowledge of wine—first, arrange a dinner with four to eight friends in a restaurant which offers an extensive list of relatively inexpensive wines (under $10 per bottle). This will give you the opportunity to taste a variety of wines at the same dinner.

Second, organize a special dinner where you bring your own wines. This, of course, requires permission and advance planning with the proprietor. For example, I recently organized a dinner-tasting of Barolo. I chose my favorite Italian restaurant (Le Alpi, New York City) and requested a special dinner to accompany these robust wines. Normally, Le Alpi prepares light, delicate dishes, but this would never do with Barolo (at least not to my palate). I persuaded the owner to offer a special dinner for the wine as well as to let us bring in our own wines.

In order to do something like this, you would have to know the restaurant and to be a good customer. But it is worthwhile when you find a good restaurant, one you are particularly satisfied with, to frequent it regularly.

Perhaps the last method offers the best possibilities to increase your wine experience—attending wine tastings. This is usually an inexpensive way to taste a variety of wines. Often, the tastings are led by a knowledgeable individual who provides information about the wines and the areas where they are produced.

Wine tastings are organized by many clubs and associations, but the best and most diverse open to the public (and not just the trade) are held by wine clubs. The largest and, to my knowledge, only truly consumer-oriented club is Les Amis du

Vin. With nearly 200 chapters across the country and over 18,000 members, they must be doing something right. This club stresses value—value in the bottle, not on the label. They publish their own journal, *Les Amis du Vin*. Each chapter is autonomous in its arrangements for wine tastings and gourmet dinners with wine. As a result, they are more responsive to the preferences of their members. In addition, they organize trips to the wine-producing regions of the world, one of the more delightful ways to obtain firsthand knowledge of wine, and offer a discount on a selected wine or wines for each month.

For further information contact:

> Les Amis du Vin
> 2302 Perkins Place, Suite W1 #202
> Silver Spring, Maryland   20910

Knowledge of wine can also be gained, as we hope has been demonstrated, by reading about wine. The following books are recommended. An asterisk (*) or a double asterisk (**) indicates a higher recommendation for the book.

Wines of Italy, Charles G. Bode
Vini Italiani, Bruno Bruni
Atlante del Chianti Classico, Enrico Bosi
Vini Tipici e Pregiati d'Italia, Roberto Capone
Great Wines of Italy, Philip Dallas
Italian Wines and Liqueurs, Renato Dettori
Wines of Italy, T. A. Layton
Principali Vitigni da Vino Cultivati in Italia, Ministero dell'Agricoltura
*Chianti: The History of Florence and Its Wines, L. Paronetto
**Wines of Italy, Cyril Ray
*D.O.C.: The New Image for Italian Wines, Bruno Roncarati

202 · The Wines of Italy

**The Food of Italy,* Waverly Root
Wines of Italy (translated from *I Vini d'Italia*), Luigi Veronelli
Signet Book of Wine, Alexis Besphaloff
World of Wine, Creighton Churchill
Liqueurs, Peter Hallgarten
Wine, Hugh Johnson
**World Atlas of Wine,* Hugh Johnson
**Encyclopedia of Wines and Spirits,* Alexis Lichine
**Encyclopedia of Wine,* Frank Schoonmaker
The Penguin Book of Wines, Allan Sichel
Disciplinari di Produzione Vini a Denominazione di Origine Controllata, Casa Editrice Scarpis

WINES COVERED BY DOC

Explanation: * has been granted a DOC and is under consideration for DOCG
+ under consideration for DOC
# applied for DOC
S granted a DOS
s applied for DOS
(1-4) this notation is used to group those wines covered under the same DOC within a given region
Following the wine name is a list of allowable qualifiers

The granting of DOCs is a continuing process. This list was complete when *The Wines of Italy* went to press.

VALLE D'AOSTA

Carema
Donnaz
Enfer d'Arvier

PIEDMONT

(1) Asti
(1) Asti Spumante
 * Barbaresco

Riserva
Riserva Speciale
Barbera d'Alba
Superiore
Barbera d'Asti
Superiore
Barbera del Monferrato
Superiore
*Barolo
Riserva
Riserva Speciale

Boca
Brachetto d'Acqui
   Spumante
(2) Caluso Passito
   Liquoroso
Colli Tortonesi
   Barbera
   Cortese
   Cortese Spumante
(3) Cortese di Gavi
Dolcetto delle Langhe
          Monregalesi
Dolcetto d'Acqui
   Superiore
Dolcetto d'Alba
Dolcetto d'Asti
Dolcetto di Diano d'Alba
Dolcetto di Dogliani
Dolcetto d'Ovada
(2) Erbaluce di Caluso
Fara
Freisa d'Asti
Freisa di Chieri
Gattinara
(3) Gavi (Cortese di gavi)
Ghemme
Grignolino d'Asti
(4) Grignolino del Casalese
(4) Grignolino del
         Monferrato
Malvasia di Castelnuovo
       Don Bosco
Malvasia di Casorzo
   d'Asti Spumante

(1) Moscato d'Asti
(1) Moscato d'Asti
       Spumante
(1) Moscato Naturale d'Asti
Nebbiolo d'Alba
Rubino di Cantavenna
Sizzano

LIGURIA

Cinqueterre
Cinqueterre-Sciacchetra
(1) Dolceacqua
   Superiore
(1) Rossese di Dolceacqua
   Superiore

LOMBARDY

Botticino
Cellatica
(1) Chiaretto
+ Colli Morenici
    Mantovani del Garda
   Bianco
   Rosato
   Rosso
Franciacorta Pinot
   Spumante
Franciacorta Rosso
Lugana
Oltrepo Pavese
   Barbacarlo
   Barbera

Bonarda
Buttafuoco
Cortese
Moscato
  Spumante
Pinot Bianco
  Spumante
Pinot Rosato
Pinot Rosso
Riesling
Sangue di Giuda
(1) Riviera del Garda Rosso
  Superiore
Tocai di San Martino
      della Battaglia
Valtellina
Valtellina Superiore
  Grumello
  Inferno
  Sassella
  Valgella

VENEZIA EUGANEA

Bardolino
  Classico
  Classico Superiore
  Superiore
Bianco di Custoza
Breganze
  Bianco
  Cabernet
    Superiore

Pinot Bianco
  Superiore
Pinot Nero
  Superiore
Rosso
Vespaiolo
  Superiore
Cabernet di Pramaggiore
Colli Berici
  Cabernet
  Garganega or Garganego
  Merlot
  Pinot Bianco
  Sauvignon
  Tocai Bianco
  Tocai Rosso
Colli Euganei
  Bianco
    Superiore
  Moscato
  Rosso
    Superiore
Gambellara
  Recioto di Gambellara
    Spumante
  Vin Santo di Gambellara
Merlot di Pramaggiore
(1) Piave
  Cabernet del Piave
  Merlot del Piave
  Tocai del Piave
  Verduzzo del Piave
(2) Prosecco di Conegliano
  Spumante

(2) Prosecco di Conegliano-
         Valdobbiadene
      Spumante
      Superiore di Cartizze
         Spumante
(2) Prosecco Valdobbiadene
         (see Prosecco di Coneg-
         liano-Valdobbiadene,
         above)
(3) Recioto Soave
      Classico
         Liquoroso
         Spumante
      Classico Superiore
         Liquoroso
         Spumante
      Liquoroso
      Spumante
      Superiore
(4) Recioto della Valpolicella
      Amarone
         Classico
         Classico Superiore
      Classico
      Classico Superiore
      Liquoroso
         Classico
         Classico Superiore
      Spumante
         Classico
         Classico Superiore
      Liquoroso
      Superiore

      Valpentena
         Liquoroso
         Spumante
         Superiore
(3) Soave
      Classico
      Classico Superiore
      Spumante
         Classico
         Classico Superiore
         Superiore
      Superiore
      Tocai di Lison
(4) Valpolicella
      Classico
      Classico Superiore
      Spumante
         Classico
         Classico Superiore
         Superiore
      Valpentena
      Superiore
      Valpentena
(1) Vini del Piave
         (see Piave, above)

TRENTINO-ALTO ADIGE

(1) Caldaro
      Casteller
(1) Lago di Caldaro
(2) Meranese
(2) Meranese di Collina

Santa Maddalena
Teroldego Rotalino
Terlano
  Pinot Bianco
  Riesling Italico
  Riesling Renano
  Sauvignon
  Sylvaner
Valle Isarco
  Müller Turgau
  Pinot Grigio
  Sylvaner
  Traminer Aromatico
  Veltliner
  Vini del Trentino
  Cabernet
  Lagrein
  Marzemino
  Merlot
  Moscato
  Pinot
  Pinot Nero
  Riesling
  Traminer Aromatico d
          Termeno
  Vino Santo

FRIULI VENEZIA GIULIA

  Aquileia
(1) Collio
    Cabernet Francese or
          Cabernet

Malvasia
Merlot
Pinot Bianco
Pinot Grigio
Pinot Nero
Riesling Italico
Sauvignon
Tocai
Traminer
(1) Collio Goriziano
    (see Collio, above)
Colli Orientali del Friuli
  Cabernet
    Riserva
  Cabernet Francese
    Riserva
  Cabernet Sauvignon
    Riserva
  Latisana
  Merlot
    Riserva
  Picolit
    Riserva
  Pinot Bianco
  Pinot Grigio
  Pinot Nero
    Riserva
  Refosco Nostrano dal
        Peduncolo Rosso
    Riserva
  Ribolla
  Riesling Renano
  Sauvignon

Tocai
  Friulano
Verduzzo
  Friulano
Grave del Friuli
  Cabernet
  Cabernet Francese
  Cabernet Sauvignon
  Merlot Friulano
  Peduncolo Rosso
  Pinot Bianco
  Pinot Grigio
  Refosco
    Nostrano
  Tocai
  Verduzzo
    Friulano
Isonzo
  Cabernet
  Malvasia Istriana
  Merlot
  Pinot Bianco
  Pinot Grigio
  Riesling Renano
  Sauvignon
  Tocai
  Traminer Aromatico
  Verduzzo Friulano

EMILIA-ROMAGNA

Albana di Romagna
  Spumante

Gutturnio dei Colli
          Piacentini
Lambrusco Grasparossa
          di Castelvetro
Lambrusco Salamino
          di Santa Croce
Lambrusco Sorbara
Lambrusco Reggiano
Sangiovese di Romagna
  Riserva
  Riserva Speciale
Trebbiano di Romagna
  Spumante
+ Trebbiano Val di Trebbia
  Vini Colli Bolognesi
  Barbera
  Bianco dell'Abbazia
  Cabernet
  Merlot
  Pinot Bianco
  Riesling Italico
  Sauvignon

MARCHE

Bianchello del Metauro
Falerio dei Colli Ascolani
Rosso Conero
Rosso Piceno
  Superiore
Sangiovese dei Colli
          Pesaresi
Verdicchio dei Castelli
          di Jesi

Classico
Spumante
Verdicchio di Matelica
Vernaccia di Serrapetrona

TUSCANY

Bianco di Pitigliano
(1) Bianco della Parrina
Bianco Vergine Val
di Chiana
S Bianco Pisano S. Torpe
s Bianco di Cortona
s Bianco Val d'Arbia
* Brunello di Montalcino
Riserva
Chianti
Classico
Riserva
Vecchio
Colli Arentini
Colli Fiorentini
Colli Pisane
Colli Senesi
Montalbano
Rufino
(2) Elba Bianco
Spumante
(2) Elba Rosso
Montecarlo Bianco
Rosso Colline Lucchesi
(1) Rosso della Parrina
Vernaccia di S.
Gimignano

Riserva
Vin Santo Toscano
* Vino Nobile di
Montepulciano
Riserva

UMBRIA

Colli del Trasimeno
Bianco
Rosso
Orvieto
Classico
Torgiano
Bianco
Rosso

LAZIO

(1) Affile
Aleatico di Gradoli
Liquoroso
S Aprilia Bianco
S Aprilia Rosso
Cerveteri
Rosato
Rosso
(2) Cesanese del Piglio
(1) Cesanese di Affile
(3) Cesanese di Olevano
Colli Albani
Superiore
Colli Lanuvini
(4) Colonna

Cori
  Bianco
  Rosso
Est! Est!! Est!!! di
        Montefiascone
Frascati
  Spumante
  Superiore
Marino
Merlot di Aprilia
(4) Montecompatri
(4) Montecompatri-Colonna
(3) Olevano Romano
(2) Piglio
Sangiovese di Aprilia
Velletri
  Bianco
  Rosso
Zagarolo

CAMPANIA

Greco di Tufo
  Spumante
Ischia
  Bianco
    Superiore
  Rosso
Solopaca
  Bianco
  Rosato
  Rosso.
    Superiore

Taurasi
  Riserva

ABRUZZO-MOLISE

Montepulciano
        d'Abruzzo
  Vecchio
    Cerasuolo
Trebbiano

CALABRIA

Cirò
  Bianco
  Rosato
  Rosso
    Classico
    Riserva
      Classico
  Donnici
Moscato di Cosenza
  Pollino
  Savuto

APULIA

Aleatico di Puglia
  Dolce Naturale
  Liquoroso Dolce
        Naturale

Castel del Monte
Bianco
Rosato
Rosso
Riserva
Locorotondo
(1) Martina
(1) Martina Franca
Matino
Rosato
Rosso
Moscato di Trani
Dolce Naturale
Liquoroso
Ostuni Bianco
Ostuni Ottavianello
Primitivo di Manduria
S Rosato del Salento
Rosso di Cerignola
San Severo
Bianco
Spumante
Rosato
Rosso

BASILICATA

Aglianico del Vulture
Spumante
Vecchio
\# Moscato del Vulture
Spumante

SICILY

(1) Alcamo
(1) Bianco Alcamo
Cerasuolo di Vittoria
Etna
Bianco
Superiore
Rosato
Rosso
Marsala
Fine
Speciale
Superiore
Vergine
Malvasia di Lipari
Moscato di Noto
Moscato di Pantelleria
Naturale
Passito
Moscato di Siracusa

SARDINIA

\# Cannonau di Dorgali
\# Cannonau di Oliastra
\# Cannonau di Oliena
Cannonau di Sardegna
Amabile
Dolce
Secco
Superiore
Amabile

Dolce

Secco

\# Cannonau di Sarrabus

\# Cannonau di Sorso

\# Carignano del Sulcis

Girò di Cagliari

   Dolce Naturale

      Liquoroso

   Liquoroso Secco

   Secco

Malvasia di Bosa

   Dolce Naturale

      Liquoroso

   Liquoroso Secco

   Secco

Malvasia di Cagliari

   Dolce Naturale

      Liquoroso

   Liquoroso Secco

   Secco

Monica di Cagliari

   Dolce Naturale

      Liquoroso

   Liquoroso Secco

   Secco

Monica di Sardegna

Moscato di Cagliari

   Dolce Naturale

      Liquoroso

+ Moscato di Campidano

+ Moscato di Sardegna

Moscato di Sorso Sennori

Nasco di Cagliari

   Dolce Naturale

      Liquoroso

   Liquoroso Secco

   Secco

Nuragus di Cagliari

Vermentino di Gallura

Vernaccia di Oristano

APPENDIX I: STATISTICAL INFORMATION

UNITED STATES IMPORTS, MAJOR ITALIAN WINES
(Quantities in Cases)

	1972	1973	1974
Asti Spumante	n.a. *	305,896	392,730
Barbaresco	5,536	3,944	2,777
Barbera d'Alba	n.a.	7,730 [1]	1,425
Barbera d'Asti	n.a.	n.a.	3,667
Bardolino	135,983	216,268	218,475
Barolo	16,247	15,471	15,408
Brunello di Montalcino	n.a.	n.a.	500
Chianti	749,866 [2]	636,313 [2]	373,258
Chianti Classico	n.a.	n.a.	149,398
Frascati	17,775	25,815	30,874
Gattinara	n.a.	n.a.	4,650
Lambrusco	771,110	1,374,272	1,870,754
Lambrusco D.O.C.	7,305	82,470	77,645
Marino	n.a.	n.a.	52,476
Orvieto	13,161	n.a.	25,735
Soave	101,476	247,117	242,737
Valpolicella	151,228	298,259	281,419
Verdicchio	n.a.	n.a.	94,707

Source: Export certificates of analysis issued by Italian Foreign Trade Institute (I.C.E.) reported by BANFI

* Not available.
[1] Includes Barbera d'Asti.
[2] Includes Chianti Classico.

APPENDIX II

ITALIAN WINE PRODUCTION BY REGION

	1973	Estimated 1974
Piedmont	4,851,700	4,743,000
Valle d'Aosta	36,600	35,000
Lombardy	2,413,500	2,296,000
Trentino-Alto Adige	1,712,300	1,400,000
Veneto	10,268,900	8,316,000
Fruili Venezia Giulia	1,460,500	1,085,000
Liguria	416,600	420,000
Emilia-Romagna	10,306,400	9,051,000
Tuscany	4,604,100	4,956,000
Umbria	866,600	896,000
Marche	2,427,800	2,240,000
Lazio	5,120,900	5,040,000
Abruzzi	2,794,800	1,946,000
Molise	350,600	280,000
Campania	3,263,100	3,255,000
Apulia	11,633,300	9,800,000
Basilicata	496,700	455,000
Calabria	1,066,700	1,255,000
Sicily	10,183,200	8,844,000
Sardinia	2,441,700	2,765,000
Total	76,716,000	69,048,000

Quantities in hectoliters.
One hectoliter = 26.46 U.S. gallons

ITALIAN WINE PRODUCTION BY REGION
(in Hectoliters)

	1972
Piedmont	2,858,000
Valle d'Aosta	28,500
Liguria	327,600
Lombardy	1,641,000
Trentino-Alto Adige	1,254,600
Veneto	9,526,900
Friuli Venezia Giulia	1,197,200
Emilia-Romagna	8,195,700
Marche	1,670,400
Toscany	3,434,000
Umbria	645,000
Lazio	3,266,400
Campania	2,717,300
Abruzzi	2,471,600
Molise	210,600
Apulia	8,694,400
Basilicata	436,200
Calabria	959,000
Sicily	8,652,700
Sardinia	1,002,900

Total 1972 production: 59.2 million
Total 1973 production: 76.7 million
Total 1974 production: 69 million

Source: Italian Trade Commission

GLOSSARY OF ITALIAN TERMS

ABBOCCATO—semisweet

ALL'ANNATA—of the year

AMABILE—semisweet, but a little sweeter than *abboccato*

AMARO—bitter

ANNATA—vintage

ANNO DI RACCOLTO—year of the vintage

ANNO DI VENDEMMIA—year of the vintage

APERITIVO—apéritif

AQUA VITAE—brandy (water of life)

ASCIUTTO—dry

AUTOCLAVE—charmat process (tank fermentation), resulting in the bubbles in some *spumantes* or other sparkling wine

AZIENDA VINICOLA—wine company

BIANCO—white

BOTTIGLIA—bottle

CANTINA SOCIALE—cooperative

CAVATAPPI—corkscrew

CERASUOLO—cherry red (rosé)

CONSORZIO—a voluntary association of vintners formed to protect or improve the reputation of their wine by setting standards of production—they award a seal, usually a neck label, to those growers who meet the standards, the most famous being the black rooster of the Classico Chianti Consorzio

DOLCE—sweet (cannellino)

ETICHETTA—label

ETICHETTA A COLLARA—neck label

ETICHETTA A COLLARINO—neck label

FIASCHI—pear-shaped bottles covered with straw baskets which contain Chianti

FRIZZANTE—slightly sparkling

FRIZZANTINO—a prickle on the tongue

GOVERNO—the system used on Chianti and some other wines, whereby a contrived secondary fermentation is used to increase the freshness of the wine; this system is only used on those wines meant to be drunk young

LIQUORE—liqueur

LIQUOROSO—rich, sweet dessert wine

MARCO GALLO—black rooster, symbol of Classico Chianti

MODO BIANCO—the white way, vinified in white as of red grapes

NERO—black

ORECCHIO—ear (of the grape bunch)

PASSITO—made from grapes dried before fermenting

POSITO—pink (rosé)

RINFRESCATORO—glass carafe containing a pocket for crushed ice

ROSATO—rosé

ROSE—pink (rosé)

ROSSO—red

SECCO—dry

SPUMANTE—sparkling

STRAVECCHIO—very old

UVA PASSITA—dried grape

VECCHIO—old

VENDEMMIA—vintage

VINELLO—low-alcohol (little) wine

VINI—wine (plural)

VINI PREGIATI—fine wines

VINO—wine (singular)
VINO APERTO—open wine
VINO DA PASTO—table wine
VINO DA TAGLIO—cutting wine (for blending)
VINO DEL PAESE—local wine
VINO DI LUSSO—deluxe wine
VINO FORTIFICATO—fortified wine
VINO LOCALE—local wine

INDEX

Colli Senesi, 102, 103, 105
Colline del Garda, 56, 59
Colline Pisane, 102, 103
Collio Goriziano, 85-6
Colomba Platino, 145
Colombini, 105
Colonna Roma, 126
Colorino grapes, 100
Comitato Nazionale per la Tutela delle Denominazioni d'Origine, 18, 19
Conegliano, 77
Consorzii, of Chianti, 19, 102-4; seal of, 19
Consorzio, for Segesta wine, 144
Consorzio per la Difesa dei Vini Tipici: Barolo e Barbaresco, 32; Moscato d'Asti e Asti Spumante, 29
Consorzio per la Difesa del Vino Tipico di: Chianti, 102; Orvieto, 115
Consorzio per la Tutela del Vino Marsala, 150
Cora brothers, 41
Cordial, *see* Liquore
Corniglia, 54
Cortaccia, 67
Cortese, 39, 51
Corvina Veronese grapes, 74, 75
Corvo, 145
Corvo Ala, 145
Costante, 105
Costernano, 75
Côte Rôtie, 193
Côtes du Provence Rosé, Italian equivalent of, 197
Côtes du Rhône, 28, 33, 34
Country wines, 158-64; French, Italian equivalents of, 198
Courmayeur, 25
Croatina grapes, 56, 57
Crotone, 141
Cuneo, 28, 29, 32, 34, 38
Cynar, 20, 165-7

Datini, Francesco, 100
Denominazioni di Origine Controllata, 18

Dessert, wine with, 31, 38-40, 55, 74, 77, 88, 93, 108, 147, 155-6, 189-90
Diano d'Alba, 31
DOC, 18, 19, 26, 27, 30, 32-6, 57-9, 70, 73-7, 85-8, 91-3, 102, 105, 115-16, 118-19, 122, 124, 134, 137-9, 141, 144, 145, 151, 155-7, 203-12
DOCG, 18, 19, 33, 203
Dolce, see Sweet
Dolceacqua, 54
Dolcetto, 39-40, 50, 54
Donnaz, 27
Dora Baltea Valley, 25
DOS, 18, 19, 203
Drupeggio grapes, 115
Dry wines, 26, 31-42, 45-62, 68-71, 73-9, 82, 86-8, 91-6, 103, 105, 106, 108, 114-15, 118-19, 122, 124-8, 130, 133-5, 138-41, 144-6, 148, 150, 155, 157, 176-80, 182
Duca di Salaparuta, 145
Durante, Francesco di Giovanni di, 100-1

Eggplant, wine with, 146
Egna, 67
Emilia-Romagna, 91-6, 168, 208
Enologica Valtellinese, 58
Est! Est!! Est!!! di Montefiascone, 19, 124-5, 130, 135
Etna, 145
Etna Vecchio, 146
Etnei di Mezza Montagna, 146
Euganean hills, 73

Faenza, 92
Fara, 37
Faro, 146
Farrusi, Dr. Cirilio, 138
Fascia Rossa, 137
Fassati, 107
Fiaschi, 101, 218
Fior d'Alpi, 167-8
Fish, wines with, 26, 39, 55, 59, 67-71, 74, 77, 86-8, 92-4, 115, 116, 118, 119, 122, 125, 128, 134, 135, 146, 157, 180-2
Florence, 102, 108, 109
Floridia, 144